THE ARIZONA
ANTIQUE DIRECTORY
(Second Edition)

A Statewide Guide to
Antiques and Collectibles

By Debbie Stone

Second Edition

ISBN:0-9615549-1-6

Produced by:
Arizona Antique Directory
943 W. Keating
Mesa, Arizona   85202

Printed in the United States of America

*To Ryan...who also had "hard work" to do
and to Carly...who was always so patient.*

CONTENTS...

FOR YOUR INFORMATION:

Cities and towns are listed alphabetically in this Directory. Shops within cities are also listed alphabetically. In large areas, such as Phoenix and Tucson, the cities have been divided into clusters of stores. Map locator numbers at the bottom of listings refer to maps for the city or town where the dealer is located or the nearest city or town to dealer. Usually maps are adjacent to listings, though sometimes dealers may be indicated on a map for a different city or town. If no map locator number is provided, refer to the Area of Directory Coverage Map near the front of the Directory for location of town.

CALL FIRST!
Some stores change their hours or may have erratic schedules. Call ahead to confirm hours. Please note all area codes are (602) unless otherwise listed.

Some listings may lack information if not provided by the dealer.

While every effort has been made to provide accurate information in all listings, the author cannot guarantee all facts are correct and cannot be held liable for inconvenience or expenses incurred because of inaccurate information.

SPECIAL NOTE:
Directory listings and map locators are free. If you know of other dealers or of any additional antiquing information that you think should be included in the Directory, please write:

The Arizona Antique Directory
943 W. Keating
Mesa, AZ 85202

COMMENTS FROM READERS...

"...very informative publication."

"...we really enjoyed *THE 1984 ARIZONA ANTIQUE DIRECTORY.*"

"We have followed it all over the state."

"...as a collector, I was sure glad when we found our copy."

"...thank you again for taking the time and energy to write this book."

"...you've tackled an insurmountable task and succeeded...congratulations."

THE ARIZONA ANTIQUE DIRECTORY
943 W. KEATING
MESA, AZ   85202

Please send me _____ copies of the Arizona Antique Directory at $4.50 each (includes tax and postage). My check has been made payable to THE ARIZONA ANTIQUE DIRECTORY.

Name _____

Address _____

City_____ State _____ Zip_____

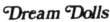

AREA OF DIRECTORY COVERAGE...

Cities and towns marked on this map have antique dealers listed in this directory.

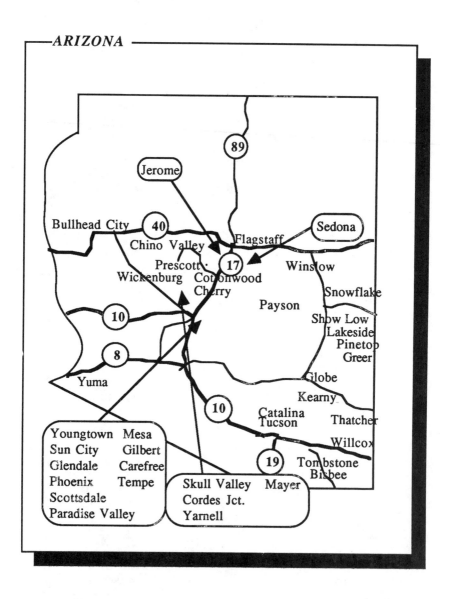

ARIZONA

Jerome

89

Bullhead City

40

Chino Valley

Flagstaff

Sedona

Prescott

17

Winslow

Wickenburg   Cottonwood
Cherry

Snowflake

Payson

Show Low
Lakeside
Pinetop
Greer

10

8

Yuma

Globe

Kearny

10

Catalina
Tucson

Thatcher

Willcox

Youngtown   Mesa
Sun City   Gilbert
Glendale   Carefree
Phoenix   Tempe
Scottsdale
Paradise Valley

19

Tombstone
Bisbee

Skull Valley   Mayer
Cordes Jct.
Yarnell

BISBEE

Colonial House Antiques-Nel Peel, Owner
20 Naco Rd., Old Bisbee, AZ 85603
432-3792   Open daily 10-5 or by appt.
Unusual collection.

Glenn McBride Fine Antiques
61 Main St., Bisbee, AZ 85603
432-4546   Open daily 10-6
Upholstery, refinishing and certified appraisals.
BISBEE MAP LOCATOR #1

On Consignment in Bisbee
On the traffic circle, Bisbee, AZ 85603
432-4002   Open M-Sa 10-6
Furniture, china, glassware, tools, appliances, household items.
BISBEE MAP LOCATOR #2

Southwest Trading
130 Tombstone Canyon, Bisbee, AZ 85603
432-7469   Open M,W,Th 10-6, F,Sa 10-9, Su 12-6
Antique, art, fun stuff and collectibles. Buy, sell or trade.
BISBEE MAP LOCATOR #3

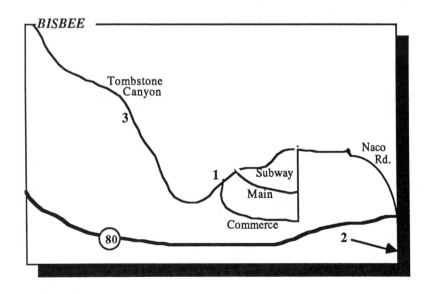

BULLHEAD CITY (RIVIERA)

B & B Antiques
436 Marina Blvd., Riviera, AZ   86442
758-1513
BULLHEAD CITY (RIVIERA) MAP LOCATOR #4

Ranch House Antiques
705 E. Marina Blvd., Riviera, AZ   86442
758-3871   Open by appt. only
General line, old pressed glass and sun purpled.
BULLHEAD CITY (RIVIERA) MAP LOCATOR #5

Trails Past Antiques
834 Hancock Rd., Riviera, AZ   86442
758-5146   Open daily 10-5
General line.
BULLHEAD CITY (RIVIERA) MAP LOCATOR #6

CAREFREE

Bradbury's Antiques-George & June Bradbury, Owners
20 Easy St., Carefree, AZ   85377
1/2 block W of the sundial.
488-3894   Open M-Sa 10-5, Su 12-5
Oriental antiques, English, European and American period furniture.
CAREFREE MAP LOCATOR #7

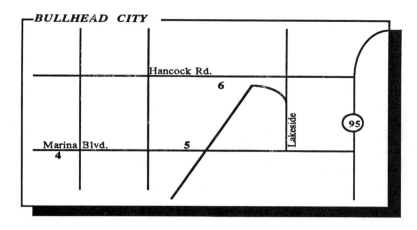

CAREFREE (cont.)

The Collector-Carollynn Jones de Szendeffy, Owner
42 Easy St., Carefree, AZ 85377
488-2313   Open M-Sa 10-5, Su 12-5
Collectibles, china, glass and furniture.
CAREFREE MAP LOCATOR #8

Tried & True Antiques-Joy Culver, Owner
CAREFREE MAP LOCATOR #9

CATALINA

Sybil's Antiques-Bill & Sybil Church, Owners
16302 N. Oracle Rd., Catalina, AZ 85738
15 miles N of Ina Rd. on Hwy 89.
825-9494   Open Tu-Sa 10-5:30
Furniture, glassware, collectibles. Friendly, unique store. Come and browse.

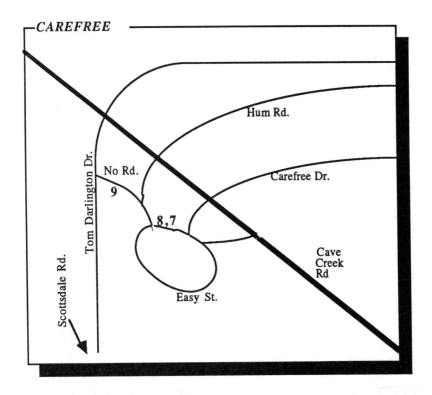

CHANDLER

The Red Barn-Kender Jones, Owner
585 N. Arizona Ave., Chandler, AZ 85224
Near SE corner of Galveston and Arizona Ave.
963-3697   Open M-Sa 10-5
A wide selection of antique and collectible furniture plus glassware from New
York and Pennsylvania. *See ad on page 13.*
CHANDLER MAP LOCATOR #10

SuDee's Antiques-SuDee & John Burris, Owners
809 N. Arizona Ave., Chandler, AZ 85224
Next door to the Village Inn.
963-6901 or 963-6234   Open M-F 10-5, Summer 10-2
Oak, pine, primitives, clocks, china, quilts. Antiques to please all collectors.
CHANDLER MAP LOCATOR #11

CHERRY

Cherry Antiques
Hwy 169, Cherry, AZ 86333
16 miles E of Dewey off Hwy 169.
Open daily 10-5.
Take the back roads to Cherry and discover the old treasures of Cherry Antiques.
MAYER MAP LOCATOR #12

CHANDLER

	Alma School Rd.		Arizona Ave.
Warner Rd.			
Ray Rd.			
		Galveston	11
Williams Field Rd.			10

CHINO VALLEY

Balance of Time Antiques-J. Wayne Roberts, Owner
545 Hwy 89, Chino Valley, AZ 86323
636-2345   Open M-Sa 9-6
Weighing devices, scales, clocks, coin operated.

Bargain House Antiques-Rog & Gerry Leyendecker, Owners
Hwy 89 N., Chino Valley, AZ 86323
20 minutes N from Prescott.
Evenings 636-2169   Open Tu-Sa

CORDES JUNCTION

Cordes Jct. Antiques-Mark & Cheryl Dishon, Owners
1901 Stagecoach Trail, Cordes Junction, AZ
In Cordes Jct. at I-17.
632-9741   Open F-M 10-5
Custom made furniture, gifts, wood primitives, old books and collectibles.
MAYER MAP LOCATOR #13

COTTONWOOD

Antiques 'N Things
1421 E. 89A, Cottonwood, AZ 86326
Verde Valley Plaza.
634-2339
Collectibles, Indian relics and gifts.
COTTONWOOD MAP LOCATOR #14

Closet Antiques-Howard & Ruth Rieke, Owners
913 N. Main St., Cottonwood, AZ 86326
In "Old Town" Cottonwood; one block N of police station.
634-3836   Open M-Sa 10:30-5
Oak furniture, Victorian furniture, glassware, china, collectibles, primitives,
pictures, books, quilts, records, duck decoys.
COTTONWOOD MAP LOCATOR #15

John's Antiques
419 E. Main St., Cottonwood, AZ 86326
At the entrance to Dead Horse Ranch State Park.
634-6424 or 634-6339   Open W-Sa 10-4:30 or by appt.
General line.
COTTONWOOD MAP LOCATOR #16

The Love Company Antiques-Bob & Judy Love, Owners
1628 E. Mingus Ave., Cottonwood, AZ 86326
634-5457   Open Tu-Sa 11-5
Primitives, trade beads and flow blue.
COTTONWOOD MAP LOCATOR #17

Red Lantern Antiques-Bob & Fran Flick, Owners
1006-08 N. Main St., Cottonwood, AZ 86326
634-7800   Open Tu-Sa 10-5 or by appt.
Over 50 categories including banks, bookends, door stops, medical instruments,
paper Americana, scales, etc.
COTTONWOOD MAP LOCATOR #18

FLAGSTAFF

Antique and Sun-Tim & Nanci, Owners
217 S. San Francisco St., Flagstaff, AZ 86001
3 blks S of Santa Fe Ave.
774-0075   Open Tu-Sa 10:30-5:30
Affordable (i.e., inexpensive) and useable antique furniture. *See ad on page 17.*
FLAGSTAFF LOCATOR #19

Black Barts Antiques & General Store
2760 E. Butler Ave., Flagstaff, AZ 86001
Across from Little America Luxury Motel at I-40 & Butler.
774-1912   Open M-Sa 10-6, Su 12-5
Lovely cut glass, art glass, oriental pieces, furniture, primitives, quilts and much more.
FLAGSTAFF MAP LOCATOR #20

Camille's Vintage Clotherie-Lynne Baker, Owner
10 1/2 N. Leroux St., Flagstaff, AZ 86001
2 blks E of the underpass and the main turnoff to Grand Canyon.
774-7516   Open Tu-F 10-5, Sa 10-4
Fine, memorable apparel, costumes, accessories including: shoes, handbags, hats and jewelry. Selected country antiques, linens. *See ad on page 16.*
FLAGSTAFF MAP LOCATOR #21

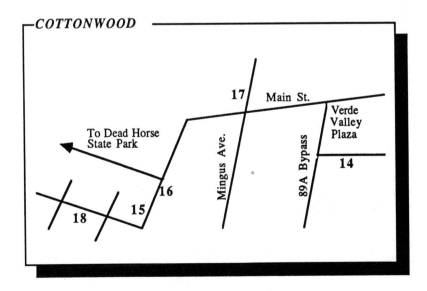

House of Antiques-Billie Caldwell, Owner
2708 N. 4th St., Suite E4, Flagstaff, AZ 86001
Knoles Village Square.
526-6368   Open M-Sa 10-5
Country oak and primitive pine furniture plus kitchen collectibles, special orders. Buy, sell, trade, consignment, estate sales.
FLAGSTAFF MAP LOCATOR #22

Red Pony Antiques-Rowena & Bob Topp, Owners
215 N. Humphreys, Flagstaff, AZ 86001
Next to the American Legion Bldg. in a charming little antique home.
774-0079   Open M-Sa 11-5 or by appt.
Selected antiques at sensible prices. A wide range of items for all ages.
FLAGSTAFF MAP LOCATOR #23

The Swan
504 N. Humphreys, Flagstaff, AZ 86001
FLAGSTAFF MAP LOCATOR #24

FLAGSTAFF (cont.)

Trifles and Treasures-Olympia Morales, Owner
2521 N. 3rd St., Flagstaff, AZ 86001
Corner of 3rd St. and Rose
Home 779-0163 Open Tu-Sa 11-4
Specializing in early American country, antiques, depression glass, pottery, fine china and collectibles, quilts, and furniture. *See ad on page 16.*
FLAGSTAFF MAP LOCATOR #25

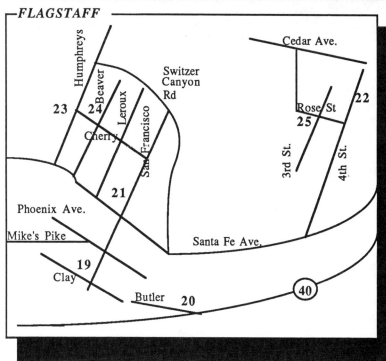

GILBERT

Country Station
130 N. Gilbert Rd., Gilbert AZ 85234
SW corner of railroad tracks and Gilbert Rd.
892-8762   Open Tu-Sa 10-4
Country crafts and antiques.

GLENDALE

Alice's Things-Alice & John, Owners
7142 N. 58th Ave., Glendale, AZ 85301
2 blks N of Glendale Ave. on 58th Ave.
931-1519 or 995-1726   Open M-Sa
Primitives, old quilts, kitchen items, post cards, collectibles, old baskets,
quilting lessons and supplies, bottles and rusty junk.
GLENDALE MAP LOCATOR #26

Annie's Antiques-Mike Generalli, Owner
6836 N. 58th Dr., Glendale, AZ 85301
NW corner Grand Ave. and 58th Dr.
931-6366   Open M-Sa 10-5
5000 square feet of showroom; radios, Edison players, jukeboxes, oak, cherry.
22 dealers. *See ad on page 19.*
GLENDALE MAP LOCATOR #27.

Antiques & Things-Jim, Owner
5915 W. Glendale Ave., Glendale, AZ 85301
W corner of 59th/Glendale/Grant
842-1380   Open M-F 8-5
Stripping, refinishing furniture.
GLENDALE MAP LOCATOR #28

Big Bear Antiques-Phil Okuma, Owner
5617 W. Maryland Ave., Glendale, AZ 85301
Antique shop on the W side of the barn behind the white house.
937-1560   Open by appt. only.
Oak furniture and Americana.
GLENDALE MAP LOCATOR #29

Country House Antiques
8625 W. Olive Ave., Glendale, AZ 85305
S side of Olive between 83rd and 91st Aves.
979-3796   Open Tu-Sa 10-4, Su by appt.
Antique furniture, crafts-quite a variety!
GLENDALE MAP LOCATOR #30

Elbo Antiques-Elli & Bo, Owners
5605 W. Glendale Ave., Glendale, AZ 85301
Next to Sargents Market. Parking on the side on 56th Ave.
842-0220   Open Tu-Sa 11-5
Advertising, neons, nostalgia, art deco, early Hollywood, toys, fun collectibles, tasteful trash for all ages. *See ad below.*
GLENDALE MAP LOCATOR #31

GLENDALE (cont.)

Kachina Indian Jewelry & Antiques
6411 W. Glendale Ave., Glendale, AZ 85301
In the Westdale Plaza Shopping Center.
247-4033   Open Tu-Sa 10-5
Indian collectibles, various antiques and furniture.
GLENDALE MAP LOCATOR #32

GLOBE

Ghost Mine Antiques
918 N. Broad St., Globe, AZ 85501
425-5150   Open by appt. only.
Primitives, glass, mining items.
GLOBE MAP LOCATOR #33

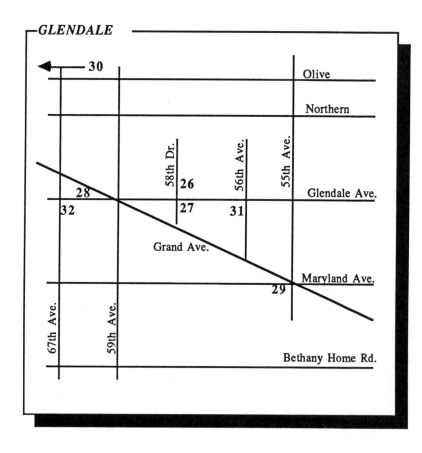

GLOBE (cont.)

Pat & Ann's Tiques
300 N. Broad St., Globe, AZ 85501
425-2863   Open Tu-Sa 10-5 (Except summer)
Furniture, glassware.
GLOBE MAP LOCATOR #34

2nd Time Around
356 Cuprite, Globe, AZ 85501
425-6228   Open by appt. only.
Kerosene lamps, a little bit of everything.
GLOBE MAP LOCATOR #35

Wagon Wheel Antiques-Betty McDonald, Owner
Wheatfields, Globe, AZ 85501
6 miles N on Apache Trail toward Roosevelt Lake.
425-1361   Open W-Su 10-5:30
Antique furniture a specialty. Glassware, lamps and misc.
GLOBE MAP LOCATOR #36

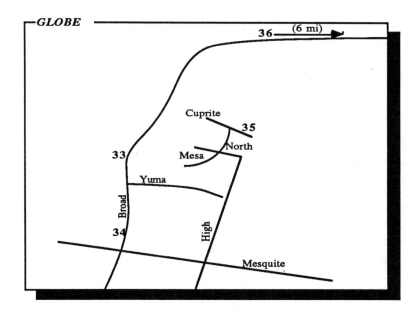

GREER

The Quacker Barrel-Judy Barger, Owner
Greer, AZ
Located next to Molly Butler Lodge on Main St.
735-7382   Open Tu-Sa 10-5, Su 10-3
Antiques, primitives, glassware, furniture, gifts and collectibles.
SNOWFLAKE MAP LOCATOR #37

JEROME

Ghost Town Antiques-Margaret Mason, Owner
Main St., Jerome, AZ 86331
Turn rt at stop sign in middle of Jerome, 5th store on rt.
634-5325   Open Tu-Th 11-4, Sa-Su 10-5
Specializing in glass, including suncolored and turn of the century glass, china, small antiques.

Tifft & Bertalan-Lyman Tifft & Erno Bertalan, Owners
329 Main St., Jerome, AZ 86331
634-9425 or 634-4914   Open daily 10-5
Glass, china, silver, estate jewelry and primitives.

KEARNY

The Brass Bell-Elizabeth Tucker
1114 Tilbury, Kearny, AZ 85237
363-7392   Open by appt. only.

LAKESIDE

Fisherman's Wife-Helen Morey & Marcia Harrison
Rt. 260, Lakeside, AZ 85929
Across from Lakeside Market.
368-6563   Open Th-Tu 10-5
Costumes, vintage clothing, antiques and collectibles.
SNOWFLAKE MAP LOCATOR #38

Harvest Moon Antiques-Kurt & Toni Augustine
Lakeside, AZ 85929
Next to LaCasa Moya Restaurant.
368-6973   Open W-Su 10:30-5:30
Antique restoration, refinishing and upholstery, fine antique furniture and stained glass.
SNOWFLAKE MAP LOCATOR #39

LAKESIDE (cont.)

K-Pierce Antiques
Main St., Lakeside, AZ 85929
Next to Homestead Cafe.
Open Th-Tu 10-5
General line.
SNOWFLAKE MAP LOCATOR #40

Pandora's Box
Lakeside, AZ 85929
Next to Cashway Lumber in Lakeside.
537-7590   Open year round.
Antiques, collectibles, furniture, Depression glass and country items.
SNOWFLAKE MAP LOCATOR #41

MAYER

Apple's Antiques-Dick & Iris Apple, Owners
Hwy 69, Mayer, AZ 86333
1 1/2 miles S of Mayer.
632-9223 or 632-7375   Open Th-Sa 10-5, Su 12-5
Large barn full; furniture, oak, pine primitives, stoves, glass, farm antiques,
uniques indoor-outdoor decorator delights.
MAYER MAP LOCATOR #42

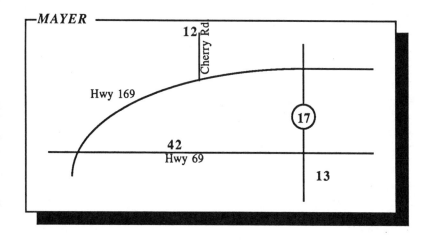

MESA

Accredited Appraisers, Ltd.-Anne & Bob Nelson
Mesa, AZ
832-5300
Appraisals only.

Brown House Antiques-Donna Johnson, Owner
141 W. 1st Ave., Mesa, AZ 85202
One blk S of Main St.
969-5823   Open M-W & F-Sa 11-3
A neat old house filled to the brim with great antiques.
MESA MAP LOCATOR #43

Collectors Corner Antiques-Suzanne & Ben Tenney
919 E. Broadway Rd.-rear, Mesa, AZ 85204
Between Horne and Stapley behind Lori's Baby Nursery.
969-0081   Open Tu-Sa 10-4
Country pine furniture, quilts, kitchen primitives, tools, copper, brass, flow blue, clocks, glass, handwork (samplers, etc.) *See ad inside front cover.*
MESA MAP LOCATOR #44

Discount Antiques-Don Plato, Owner
1946 S. Dobson Rd. #3, Mesa, AZ 85202
NW corner of Baseline and Dobson.
838-3565   Open M-Th 10-9, F-Sa 10-10, Su 1-6
General line, mostly furniture. *See ad on page 27.*
MESA MAP LOCATOR #45

Florence's Unique Country Antiques-Florence & Ralph Welckle, Owners
910 W. Broadway Rd., Mesa, AZ 85202
969-0654   Open M-Sa 9:30-5
Primitives.
MESA MAP LOCATOR #46

The Glass Urn-Fran & Roy McClendon, Owners
456 W. Main St., Mesa, AZ 85201
833-2702   Open Tu-Sa 10-4
Matching service; Fostoria, Cambridge, Tiffin, Heisey, etc.
MESA MAP LOCATOR #47

Mesa Antique Mart

921 E. MAIN
MESA

72 DEALER SHOPS
STOCKING EVERYTHING
FROM THIMBLES TO ARMOIRES

962-6305

OPEN 9:30 / 5:30
MONDAY-SATURDAY

Antiques & Collectibles

Gray Goose Antiques
1245 W. Baseline Rd., Suite 111, Mesa, AZ 85202
SW corner of Baseline and Alma School.
345-0202 or 345-0203   Open M-Sa 10-5
General line.
MESA MAP LOCATOR #48

Mesa Antique Mart-Larry & Dee Penner, Owners
921 E. Main St., Mesa, AZ 85203
Between Horne and Stapley on Main; S side of the street.
962-6305   Open M-Sa 9:30-5:30, Th 9:30-8
72 antiques and collectibles dealers displaying everything from thimbles to
armoires. *See ad on page 25.*
MESA MAP LOCATOR #49

Ron and Soph Antiques-Ron & Sophie Williams, Owner
1060 W. Broadway Rd., Mesa, AZ 85202
E of Alma School on Broadway.
964-7437   Open W-Sa 10-5
Antique and other fine furniture, clocks, lamps, pictures, china and jewelry.
MESA MAP LOCATOR #50

Stewart's Military Antiques
P.O. Box 5106, Mesa, AZ 85201
834-4004   Open by appt. only.
Military collectibles, both U.S. and foreign, from the American Civil War
through World War II.

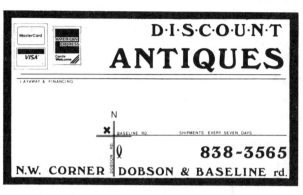

MESA (cont.)

Wood-Be-Nice
243 S. Sirrine St., Mesa, AZ 85202
N of Broadway, E of Center.
833-5185   Open M-F 8-5, Sa 8-1
Stripping and refinishing antique furniture. *See ad on page 26.*
MESA MAP LOCATOR #51

MESA

Main   47
                                    49
1st Ave
43
46   Sirrine 51
50   Broadway
                 44 Temple
                 Southern
45   Baseline
48

Dobson Alma School Extension Country Club Mesa Drive Horne Stapley

PARADISE VALLEY

Morse Studio of Interior Design Ltd.
5203 E. Lincoln Dr., Paradise Valley, AZ 85253
44th St. and Lincoln.
840-8120   Open M-F 9-5

PAYSON

Payson Antique Ranch-Rocky Baranowski, Owner
208 E. Bonita, Payson, AZ 85541
256-2008   Open daily 10-5.
Antiques, fine arts and custom framing.
PAYSON MAP LOCATOR #52

Pioneer Village Trading Post
1117 N. Beeline Hwy., Payson, AZ 85541
Next to bowling alley.
474-3911   Open M-Sa 9-5:30, Su 12-5
Cowboy, Indian and western.
PAYSON MAP LOCATOR #53

NORTH PHOENIX

Antique Alley, Inc.
12410 N. Cave Creek Rd., Phoenix, AZ 85022
NW corner or Cave Creek Rd., Cactus and Thunderbird.
867-4611   Open M, T & Sa 10-6, W-F 10-9, Su 11-5
Nostalgic marketplace for over 68 antique dealers, collectibles, slot machines, oak furniture, advertising, toys and Disneyana. *See ad on page 33.*
NORTH PHOENIX MAP LOCATOR #54

Antique Magic-Susan & Peggy
9626 N. 16th Pl., Phoenix, AZ 85020
N of Hatcher; near Cave Creek and Mtn. View
944-0386 or 867-7343   Open by appt. only.
Refinishing.

```
┌─PAYSON ─────────────────────────────────────────┐
│      Hwy 260          │53                        │
│                       │                          │
│                       │ ≩                        │
│      Bonita           │ ≛        52              │
│      Main             │ ≛                        │
│                       │ ᴮᵉᵉˡᶦⁿᵉ                  │
└─────────────────────────────────────────────────┘
```

Antique Outpost-Winn & Frank Green, Owners
10012 N. Cave Creek Rd., Phoenix, AZ 85020
1 mile N of Dunlap, Cave Creek, 7th St. intersection.
943-9594   Open M-W & F-Sa 10-5, Su 12-5
Buy and sell antiques and collectibles. Largest variety antiques and collectibles
in the valley of the sun. Here for 18 years!
NORTH PHOENIX MAP LOCATOR #55

Antique Peddlers
9214 N. Cave Creek Rd., Phoenix, AZ 85020
997-2117   Open M-Sa 10-5, Su 12-5
6 dealers featuring Depression glass, country furniture, stoneware, kitchen
gadgets and books. *See ad on page 31.*
NORTH PHOENIX MAP LOCATOR #56

Antiques Warehouse, Inc.-Irving Horwitz, Owner
9838 N. 19th Ave., Phoenix, AZ 85021
Between Hatcher & Peoria on N 19th Ave., W side of st.
944-8212   Open W-F 10-6, Sa 10:30-6
Antique and authentic oak reproduction furniture for the entire home. Kimball
Victorian furniture and brass accessories.
NORTH PHOENIX MAP LOCATOR #57

Camel Antiques-West
9838 N. 19th Ave., Phoenix, AZ 85015
Between Hatcher and Peoria on N 19th Ave.
861-1316   Open M-Sa 10-5:30
Direct importers of 18th and 19th century French furniture and accessories. *See
ad on page 39.*
NORTH PHOENIX MAP LOCATOR #58

Dennis Hill Antiques-Dennis Hill, Owner
32 W. Hatcher Rd., Phoenix, AZ 85021
944-3102   Open M-Sa 10-5
See ad on page 31.
NORTH PHOENIX MAP LOCATOR #59

e Corner-Mickie Haynes, Owner
. 7th Ave., Phoenix, AZ 85013
of Indian School.
86   Open M-Sa 10-4, Summer W-Sa 10-2
re, china, primitives, quilts, rag rugs, country things, antique dolls and
ies. 7 dealers! *See ad on page 7.*
RAL PHOENIX MAP LOCATOR #63

tique Den-Lavada & Dean Benson, Owners
7th St., Phoenix, AZ 85014
of Bethany Home Rd. on 7th St.
8   Open Tu-Sa 10-4
line of antiques and collectibles, friendly service on Antique Row. *See*
ge 35.
AL PHOENIX MAP LOCATOR #64

s Forever-Mike & Kathy Harris, Owners
12th St., Phoenix, AZ 85014
Highland.
4   Open M-Sa 10-5
zing in oak furniture, also small items, paper Americana and light
See ad on page 37.
AL PHOENIX MAP LOCATOR #65

s & Toys
Central Ave., Phoenix, AZ 85012
-Sa 11-5
oys and collectibles.
L PHOENIX MAP LOCATOR #66

Spinning Wheel-Ida Lutfy, Owner
cDowell Rd., Phoenix, AZ 85006
    Open M, W, F-Sa 1-4
L PHOENIX MAP LOCATOR #67

Historical Cache
th St., Phoenix, AZ 85014
Bethany Home Rd. on 7th St.
 10-4, Sa 9-5
ntiques and collectibles. *See ad on page 35.*
L PHOENIX MAP LOCATOR #68

NORTH PHOENIX (cont.)

In Days of Old
2841 E. Bell Rd., Phoenix, AZ 85032
SW corner of Bell Rd. and 29th St. in office plaza.
971-8553   Open M-Sa 11-5
American oak furniture, accessories, jewelry, refinishing, caning, with a
mixture of silk flowers and plants.
NORTH PHOENIX MAP LOCATOR #60

Katie's Antiques
9215 N. 8th St., Phoenix, AZ 85020
Next to Antique Peddlers.
944-6528   Open M-F 10:30-3, Sa 11:30-5, Su 12-4 & by appt.
Country, Depression glass and furniture.
NORTH PHOENIX MAP LOCATOR #61

Unique Antiques
15677 N. Cave Creek Rd., Phoenix, AZ 85032
482-9321   Open Tu-F 3-6, Sa 10-5, Su 12-5
French, English and American furniture. Refinishing and decorating services
available.
NORTH PHOENIX MAP LOCATOR #62

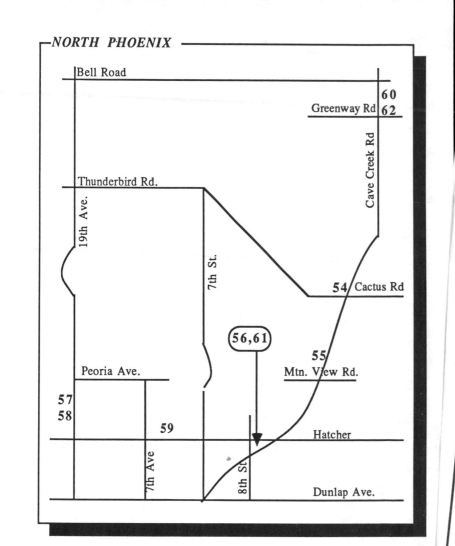

Bell Road

Greenway Rd **60**
62

Cave Creek Rd

Thunderbird Rd.

19th Ave.

7th St.

54 Cactus Rd

56,61

55
Mtn. View Rd.

Peoria Ave.

57
58

59

7th Ave

8th St.

Hatcher

Dunlap Ave.

*Largest selection of collectable
paper items in Arizona.*

Magazine covers & ads, citrus crate labels, calendars, sheet music, car ads, trade cards, stereo views, sports & movie items. Also carry a line of marcasite & reproduction jewelry.

Antique Alley Space 65
12410 N. Cave Creek Rd., Phoenix, AZ

Antique Alley INC

12410 N. Cave Creek Road
Phoenix, Arizona 85022
(602) 867-4611

A NOSTALGIC, AIR CONDITIONED MARKE
68 DEALER SPACES.

CONVENIENTLY LOCATED IN THE HOME
AT CAVE CREEK ROAD & CACTUS / THUN

<u>OPEN SEVEN DAYS A WEEK</u>, COME AND
NOSTALGIC WAY,   COUNTRY   ROAD,
AND MAIN STREET WITH U

VISA, MASTER CHARGE, AMERICAN EX

North 7th Street
Antique Row
With 5 Shops

Arizona Historical Cache

Glenn's Frame Shop 279-7501

Granny's Hideaway Antiques 264-9459

Antique Den 274-0288

Snoop Sisters 274-9285

5801 to 5809 North 7th Street
just south of Bethany Home Road

Back to the Country Antiques
2521 N. 7th St., Phoenix, AZ 85006
253-7827   Open by appt. only.
Primitives.
CENTRAL PHOENIX MAP LOCATOR #69

Bobbi's Antiques-Bobbie Phillips, Owner
3838 N. 7th St., Phoenix, AZ 85012
S of Indian School Rd.; take 7th St. N off freeway.
279-7768   Open Tu-Sa 10-5
American furniture; regular and unusual. Glassware, primitives, picture frames
and misc. Appraisals, customer refinishing.
CENTRAL PHOENIX MAP LOCATOR #70

Bradbury's Antiques-George & June Bradbury, Owners
4242 N. 7th Ave., Phoenix, AZ 85013
Next to Antique Corner.
274-3731   Open M-Sa 10-4
Largest selection of Hummels in the country; oriental and American furniture.
CENTRAL PHOENIX MAP LOCATOR #71

The Brewery-Lynn Geyer, Owner
1605 N. 7th Ave., Phoenix, AZ 85007
7th Ave. at McDowell.
252-1415   Erratic hours (call first)
Advertising, collectibles with a very strong emphasis on breweriana, neons,
tins and beer cans. Beer signs for home bars.
CENTRAL PHOENIX MAP LOCATOR #72

Camel Antiques, Ltd.
1000 E. Camelback Rd., Phoenix, AZ 85014
277-0101   Open M-Sa 10-5
Direct importers of 18th and 19th century French furniture and accessories. *See
ad on page 39.*
CENTRAL PHOENIX MAP LOCATOR #73

Celery Seed Antiques
P.O. Box 10374, Phoenix, AZ 85064
955-9508   Shows only.
General line.

The Collection-Dorothy Flood & Lola Rice, Owners
4407 N. 7th St., Phoenix, AZ 85014
On E side of 7th St. between Camelback and Indian School.
264-3131   Open Tu-Sa 9:30-4:30
Large selection of quality furniture, glass, porcelain, silver and brass. Priced to sell. Dealers welcome.
CENTRAL PHOENIX MAP LOCATOR #74

Duncan's Antiques
525 N. 1st St., Phoenix, AZ 85004
SE corner of 1st and Fillmore.
258-7778
European, American and French furniture. Bric-a-brac, lighting.
CENTRAL PHOENIX MAP LOCATOR #75

Ed & Elaine's-Ed & Elaine Shultz, Owners
4822 N. 7th St., Phoenix, AZ 85014
Between Camelback and Highland on the W side of 7th St.
279-9129   Open Tu-Sa 9-6
We recondition, repair, rejuvenate and reupholster antique and fine quality furniture. We stock old couches and chairs.
CENTRAL PHOENIX MAP LOCATOR #76

The Elms
310 E. Thomas Rd., Phoenix, AZ 85012
285-0999   Open M-Sa 9:30-4:30
Wall decor, lamps, table top decorations, antiques, select occasional furniture and oriental art.
CENTRAL PHOENIX MAP LOCATOR #77

Forget Me Knots Antique Gallery
3060 N. 16th St., Phoenix, AZ 85016
W side of 16th, N of Thomas.
266-2441   Open Tu-Sa 9-5
Strip and refinish, caning. *See ad on page 43.*
CENTRAL PHOENIX MAP LOCATOR #78

The 4 Walls-Ruth Algis, Owner
417 E. Roosevelt St., Phoenix, AZ 85004
277-1091   Open by appt. only.
Pictures, wall arrangements and picture framing.
CENTRAL PHOENIX MAP LOCATOR #79

Fry's Antiques-Gladys Fry, Owner
6821 N. 16th St., Phoenix, AZ 85016
Located in shopping center 1/2 blk S of Glendale Ave.
277-0426   Open M-Sa 10-6
Furniture, glass, primitives and collectibles. *See ad on page 41.*
CENTRAL PHOENIX MAP LOCATOR #80

Furniture Galleria
1821 E. Indian School Rd., Phoenix, AZ 85016
In the middle between 16th and 20th Sts.
277-5434   Open M-F 10-5, Sa 10-2
CENTRAL PHOENIX MAP LOCATOR #81

Glenn's Frame Shop
5801A N. 7th St., Phoenix, AZ 85014
On Antique Row.
279-7501   Open Tu-F 9:30-4:30, Sa 9-12
Custom framing, special antiques and antique frame refurbishing. *See ad on page 35.*
CENTRAL PHOENIX MAP LOCATOR #82

Granny's Hideaway Antiques-Gerald & Mary Winklepleck, Owners
5807 N. 7th St., Phoenix, AZ 85014
On Antique Row.
264-9459   Open Tu-Sa 11-4
Antique dolls, glassware, furniture and primitives. Always buying dolls, Victorian and country antiques. *See ad on page 35.*
CENTRAL PHOENIX AD LOCATOR #83

Hinkley's Lighting Co.
4620 N. Central Ave., Phoenix, AZ 85012
W side of Central between Camelback and Indian School.
279-6267   Open M-F 9-5:30, Sa 10-5
Antique lighting fixtures.
CENTRAL PHOENIX MAP LOCATOR #84

CENTRAL PHOENIX (cont.)

Jim's Antiques and Furniture
2301 N. 7th St., Phoenix, AZ 85006
NE corner of Oak and 7th St.
254-4840   Open M-Sa 9-5
6000 square feet of American antique furniture. Caning and refinishing, too.
CENTRAL PHOENIX MAP LOCATOR #85

Ledbetters Antiques
915 N. Central Ave., Phoenix, AZ 85004
SE corner of Central and Roosevelt.
257-1455   Open Tu-Sa 11-3
Since 1943: antiques and collectibles, wholesale to the public. Largest, most diversified selection in town. Estate auctioneers and appraisers.
CENTRAL PHOENIX MAP LOCATOR #86

Lillian's Antiques-Ben Feiler, Owner
609 W. Osborn Rd., Phoenix, AZ 85013
Osborn at 7th Ave.
279-9619   Open M-Sa 10-5, Summer 10-4
Furniture, bygone books, glass, china, jewelry, collectibles, clocks, watches, dolls, souvenir spoons, etc.
CENTRAL PHOENIX MAP LOCATOR #87

Millie's Antiques-Ida Lutfy, Owner
710 N. Central Ave., Phoenix, AZ 85004
254-5697   Open M-Sa 9:30-5
CENTRAL PHOENIX MAP LOCATOR #88

Old Towne Antiques-John and Melanie Towne, Owners
2605 N. 7th St., Phoenix, AZ 85006
NE corner of Virginia and 7th Sts.
266-5206   Open M-Sa 10-5
General line of turn-of-the-century oak furniture, country accessories and collectibles. *See ad on page 41.*
CENTRAL PHOENIX MAP LOCATOR #89

Resurrection Antiques & Sales Co.
810 E. Indian School Rd., Phoenix, AZ 85014
248-9325   Open M-F 9-5, Sa 10-4
American oak, Victorian walnut, stained glass, wicker, advertising, etc.
CENTRAL PHOENIX MAP LOCATOR #90

Second Hand Rose-Vic & Linda Cresto, Owners
1350 E. Indian School Rd., Phoenix, AZ 85014
266-5956   Open Tu-Sa 11-5
See ad on page 45.
CENTRAL PHOENIX MAP LOCATOR #91

Signs-Plus
121 W. Camelback Rd., Phoenix, AZ 85013
1 blk W of Central on S side of Camelback.
277-7446   Open M-F 9-5, Sa 9-1
Gas pumps, collectible signs and neon bar signs.
CENTRAL PHOENIX MAP LOCATOR #92

Snoop Sisters-Paul Banks & Sue Brown, Owners
5809 N. 7th St., Phoenix, AZ 85014
On Antique Row.
274-9285   Open M-Sa 10-4
An everchanging collection of nice old things you'd like to live with. *See ad on page 35.*
CENTRAL PHOENIX MAP LOCATOR #93

Stone House Antiques-Diane Wertz, Owner
2037 N. 7th St., Phoenix, AZ 85006
252-8391 or 952-1075   Open Tu-Sa 10-4
American period country furniture, quilts and folk art. *See ad on page 37.*
CENTRAL PHOENIX MAP LOCATOR #94

Stop'n Swap-Tom Moody, Owner
1520 E. Washington St., Phoenix, AZ 85034
N side of the street between 15th and 16th.
252-0649   Open Tu-Sa 8-5
Oldest antique and second-hand gun store in Phoenix area.
CENTRAL PHOENIX MAP LOCATOR #95

Stuff Antiques-Joe Weaver, Owner
407 E. Roosevelt St., Phoenix, AZ 85004
Middle of block between 4th and 5th Sts., S side of street.
252-0612   Open Tu-Sa 10-5
Antique lamps, light fixtures from Victorian, art nouveau, art deco. Stained and beveled windows, doors and slot machines. *See ad on page 45.*
CENTRAL PHOENIX MAP LOCATOR #96

✥STUFF✥

ANTIQUES

YOU SIMPLY WON'T BELIEVE THE OVERWHELMING VARIETY, QUALITY AND SELECTION.

SPECIALIZING IN ANTIQUE VICTORIAN, ART NOUVEAU, ART DECO LIGHTING, TABLE LAMPS, FLOOR LAMPS, CEILING LIGHTS, WALL LIGHTS.

STAINED, BEVELLED GLASS WINDOWS, DOORS.

SLOT MACHINES AND OTHER COIN OPERATED DEVICES.

SPECIALISTS IN REPAIR AND RESTORATION OF ABOVE ITEMS.

HOURS:
10-5 TUES.- SAT.   407 E. ROOSEVELT   252-0612

Second Hand Rose

**Pine, Walnut & Oak Furniture.
Country Furnishings
Wicker & Toys
Advertising Items**

EXPERT RESTORATION AVAILABLE

1350 E. Indian School Road
10 - 5 M-Sat.   266-5956

ARIZONA ANTIQUE DIRECTORY   **45**

CENTRAL PHOENIX (cont.)

Treasured Memories
311 W. Camelback Rd., Suite A, Phoenix, AZ   85013
Just W of N Central on S side of Camelback.
266-1986   Open Tu-Sa 10-4
Primitives; large selection of oak, pine and walnut furniture. Wholesale to the trade. *See ad on page 41.*
CENTRAL PHOENIX MAP LOCATOR #97

Treasures-Susan Palmer-Hunter, Owner
3448 N. 16th St., Phoenix, AZ   85016
265-3440   Open Tu-Sa 11-3
English, pine and country furniture. *See ad on page 47.*
CENTRAL PHOENIX MAP LOCATOR #98

Uptown Antiques-Frank Donnelly & John Sullivan, Owners
4411 N. 7th St., Phoenix, AZ   85014
On 7th St. between Camelback and Indian School.
266-6105 or 266-2049   Open Tu-Sa 10-5
Furniture, brass beds, beer steins, china, oriental rugs, clocks, etc.
CENTRAL PHOENIX MAP LOCATOR #99

WEST PHOENIX

Antique Ford Supply
3040 W. McDowell Rd., Phoenix, AZ   85009
E of 31st Ave., on N side of McDowell.
278-3858   Open M-F 9-6, Sa 9-4
Antique Ford parts, comic books and phonograph records.
WEST PHOENIX MAP LOCATOR #100

Antique Haven-Pat Evans, Owner
2725 W. Glendale Ave., Phoenix, AZ   85021
246-0290 or 843-2167   Open Tu-F 11-4, Sa 12-4
Antiques and collectibles. *See ad on page 53.*
WEST PHOENIX MAP LOCATOR #101

Aunt Polly's Attic
2731 W. Glendale Ave., Phoenix, AZ   85021
Next to Antique Haven.
242-3101   Open M-Sa 10-4
General line.
WEST PHOENIX MAP LOCATOR #102

English Pine
and
Country Furniture

Antique Furniture
(circa 1700-1900)
Prints, Mirrors and Accessories
Silver, Linens and Lace

New Gift Items Arriving Weekly

TREASURES

3448 N. 16th St., Phoenix, AZ 85016, (602) 265-3440
Hours: Tues.–Sat. 11-3

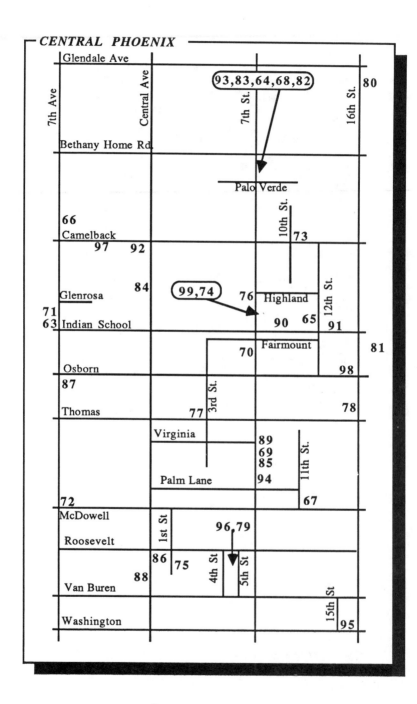

CENTRAL PHOENIX

Glendale Ave

7th Ave

Central Ave

93,83,64,68,82

7th St.

16th St.

80

Bethany Home Rd

Palo Verde

10th St.

66
Camelback

97   92

Glenrosa

84

99,74

76   Highland

73

12th St.

71
63 Indian School

90   65

91

70   Fairmount

81

Osborn

98

87

3rd St.

Thomas

77

78

Virginia

89
69
85
94

11th St.

Palm Lane

72

67

McDowell

1st St

Roosevelt

96,79

86
75

4th St

5th St

Van Buren

88

15th St

Washington

95

Cactus Patch
2625 W. Northern Ave., Phoenix, AZ   85021
864-0182   Open M-Sa 10-5
General line.
WEST PHOENIX MAP LOCATOR #103

Circa Galleries
2922 W. Weldon Ln., Phoenix, AZ   85017
234-3566   Open M-Sa 10-5, Su 12-5
Architectural and designer antiques from all over the world. Fine furnishings,
paintings, lighting, etc. Glass doors and windows.
WEST PHOENIX MAP LOCATOR #104

The Crystal Clinic-Walter F. Shaw, Owner
2827 W. Northview Ave., Phoenix, AZ   85021
864-1082   Open by appt. only.
Expert glass repair. *See ad on page 53.*
WEST PHOENIX MAP LOCATOR #105

Electrical Antique Restorations-Frank Osborn, Owner
3753 W. Becker Ln., Phoenix, AZ   85029
978-1326   Open by appt. only.
Buy, restore and sell antiques. Ceiling and desk fans plus other
electro-mechanical devices.
WEST PHOENIX MAP LOCATOR #106

The Emporium West-Jim & Rebecca Harscher, Owners
6019 N. 35th Ave., Phoenix, AZ   85017
In the West Plaza on Bethany Home Rd. at 35th Ave.
973-8897   Open M-W, F, Sa 10-6, Th 10-8
A nostalgia marketplace featuring 40 distinct shops. *See ads on pages 50, 51
& opposite inside back cover.*
WEST PHOENIX MAP LOCATOR #107

Eric's English Antiques Ltd.-Eric, Owner
2539 W. Northern Ave., Phoenix, AZ   85021
200 yards W of freeway on Northern Ave.
995-2950   Open Tu-Sa 10-5
English antiques; European and American antiques. Inexpensive English
antiques in large quantities. *See ad on page 53.*
WEST PHOENIX MAP LOCATOR #108

Your Emporium

Collector's Closet
Space #1, #26 & #29

Furniture
Copper
Glassware
Old Prints

Bull House Antiques
Space #8 & #30

Furniture
Glassware
Old Toys
Linens

Around De Corner
Space #4 & #27

Primitives
Furniture
Pottery
Quilts

Elbo Antiques
Space #16 & #17

Art Deco
Old Advertising
Neons
Beer Signs

Nancy's Place
Space #28

Kitchen Collectibles
20's, 30's & 40's
Appliances & Decorator Items
Unusual 30's & 40's Items
Clothing

Annalee's Attic
Space #3

Glassware
Furniture
Kitchen Collectibles
Depression Glass
Fine China

ART DECO
TOYS & DOLLS
OLD ADVERTISING
VINTAGE CLOTHING
FURNITURE
NEONS

THE
EMPORIUM
WEST

GLASSWARE
OLD PHONES
DEPRESSION GLASS
COLLECTOR ITEMS
DECORATOR ITEMS
PRIMITIVES

A Nostalgia Marketplace.

WEST PLAZA • 6019 NORTH 35th AVENUE • PHOENIX, ARIZONA 85017 • 602-973-8897
SUN: 12-5, MON: 10-8, TUE-SAT: 10-6, THR: 10-8

West Travel Guide

1. Collector's Closet
2. Around De Corner
3. Annalee's Attic
4. Around De Corner
5. Dixie Davis
6. Franklin's Square
7. Just Ducky
8. Bull House Antiques
9. Trinkets & Treasures
10. J. Todd & Associates
11. Profit for Profits
12. Joe Martino
13. Telephone Man
14. Wilma's Place
15. Classic Antiques
16. Elbo Antiques
17. Elbo Antiques
18. The Postcard Man
19. Portabello Road
20. Dennis Hill's Antiques
21. Antiques by Diane
22. Vintage Shop
23. Dona's Antiques
    & Estate Sales
24. Tim & Dave's Shop
25. Annies
26. Collector's Closet
27. Around De Corner
28. Nancy's Place
29. Collector's Closet
30. Bull House Antiques
31. Tim & Dave's Shop
32. New York Bound
33. Remembrance
34. Sorenson's Antiques
35. Bird In The Hand
36. Portabello Road
37. Debbie's Daze
38. Unique Antiques
39. Frannies

MALL

39	16	15
38	17	14
37	18	13
36	19	12
35	20	11
34	21	10
33	22	9
32	23	8
31	24	7
30	25	6
29	26	5
28	27	4
3		OFFICE
2		LOUNGE
40	1	

PARKING

WEST PHOENIX (cont.)

H. J. Schag Antiques
1316 W. Berridge Ln., Phoenix, AZ 85013
249-1008   Open by appt. only.

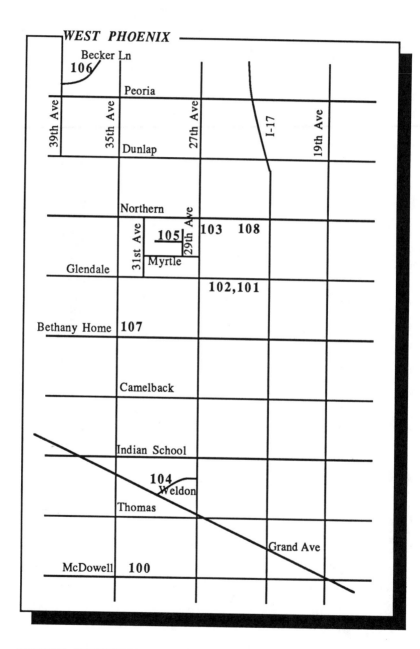

EAST PHOENIX

A & F Antiques, Hummels & Collectibles
3120 E. Indian School Rd., Phoenix, AZ 85016
954-0504
Specializing in antiques, Hummels, plates, figurines and oriental art objects.
See ad on page 55.
EAST PHOENIX MAP LOCATOR #109

Antiquarian II Book Outlet
5138 E. Thomas Rd., Phoenix, AZ
NW corner of 52nd St. and Thomas.
952-9413   Open M-Sa 11-5:30
Used and out-of-print books.
EAST PHOENIX MAP LOCATOR #110

The Antiquary-Grant & Betty Zimmerman, Owners
3044 N. 24th St., Phoenix, AZ 85016
Between Thomas and Osborn.
955-8881 or 955-7003   Open M-Sa 9-5
American and European antiques. Silver, historical Staffordshire, primitives, folk art, pottery, porcelain and collectibles.
EAST PHOENIX MAP LOCATOR #111

Classic Carriage House
5552 E. Washington St., Phoenix, AZ 85034
275-6825
Antique, classic collectible cars; Mercedes, Rolls Royce, Cadillac, etc.
Appraisals, member International Society of Appraisers.
EAST PHOENIX MAP LOCATOR #112

Do Wah Diddy-Doug & Shay Patterson, Owners
3542 E. Thomas Rd., Phoenix, AZ 85018
1 blk E of 32nd St. on the N side of Thomas.
957-3874   Open Tu-F 12-6, Sa 12-5
1930's to 1960's; art deco, moderne furniture and accessories. Movie memorabilia, comic character collectibles and antique advertising. *See ad on page 57.*
EAST PHOENIX MAP LOCATOR #113

Ellyn Tesky
4945 E. Cheery Lynn Rd., Phoenix, AZ 85018
952-9266   Open by appt. only.
Appraisals only.
EAST PHOENIX MAP LOCATOR #114

Gaslight Antiques & Junque
2511 E. McDowell Rd., Phoenix, AZ 85008
E of 24th St. on S side of McDowell.
275-7430   Open Tu-F 10:30-5, Sa 10:30-4
Glassware, clocks, furniture, pictures. General line.
EAST PHOENIX MAP LOCATOR #115

Hasbrook Interiors & Antiques, Inc.-Patricia Hasbrook, Owner
4410 E. Camelback Rd., Phoenix, AZ 85018
NE corner of Camelback and 44th St.
840-1705   Open M-F 8:30-5:30, Sa 10-5
Direct European and oriental importers.
EAST PHOENIX MAP LOCATOR #116

Honey Buns-Adelle & Miss Elli, Owners
3405 N. 24th St., Suite 1, Phoenix, AZ 85016
Upstairs, N of Osborn.
224-0767   Open M, W, F, Sa 12-5, Tu, Th 12-7
Vintage apparel for the adventurous vixen. Featuring 30's, 40's and 50's clothes. *See ad on page 57.*
EAST PHOENIX MAP LOCATOR #117

Labriola's
3311 N. 24th St., Phoenix, AZ 85016
Just S of Osborn on 24th St.
956-5370   M-Sa 11-4
French and European furniture.
EAST PHOENIX MAP LOCATOR #118

Phoenix Lamp & Silver Repair
2225 E. Indian School Rd., Phoenix, AZ 85016
955-5640   Open M-F 9-5
Antique lighting fixtures and lamps.
EAST PHOENIX MAP LOCATOR #119

EAST PHOENIX (cont.)

Rainbow Antiques-Odessa Koelsch & Mary Frances Slaughter, Owners
4520 E. Indian School Rd., Suite 3, Phoenix, AZ   85018
840-0830   Open by appt. only.
Depression glass, fiesta and collectibles.
EAST PHOENIX MAP LOCATOR #120

Richardson Antiques-Morris, Virginia & Tony Richardson, Owners
2949 N. 28th St., Phoenix, AZ   85016
1 blk N of Thomas Rd.
956-5085   Open M-Su 11-5
Oak furniture and collectibles.
EAST PHOENIX MAP LOCATOR #121

EAST PHOENIX (cont.)

Yesteryear Antiques-Grant Yeo, Owner
2125 N. 24th St., Phoenix, AZ 85008
267-9634   Open M-F 8:30-5:30, Sa 8:30-12
Oak furniture.
EAST PHOENIX MAP LOCATOR #122

PINETOP

Curiosity Shoppe-Eleanor B. Gilroy, Owner
Hwy 260, Pinetop, AZ 85935
Across from Circle K; S end of Pinetop.
367-0311   Open 10-5
Quality antiques, home and country accessories.
SNOWFLAKE MAP LOCATOR #123

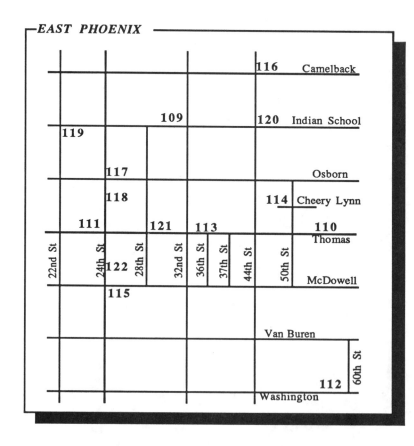

PINETOP (cont.)

Helen's Antiques-Helen D. Smigel, Owner
P.O. Box 1097, Pinetop, AZ 85935
Turn at Pinetop Realty.
367-4212   Open Memorial Day- Labor Day M-Sa 10-5
Oldest dealer in town! Glass, sterling and Victorian jewelry.
SNOWFLAKE MAP LOCATOR #124

Out-of-the-Way Antiques-Lee or Julie, Owners
P.O. Box 1486, Pinetop, AZ 85935
Hwy 260-Show Low to Pinetop; turn rt on Pinecrest Rd.
367-0943   Open daily 10-5.
Furniture, primitives, collectibles, old clothes and china.
SNOWFLAKE MAP LOCATOR #125

Pinetop Furniture & Antiques-Steve & Sandi Vanderpool, Owners
Pinetop, AZ 85935
Next to Pinetop Country Store.
367-5757   Open M-Sa 9:30-6
Wide range of antiques and collectibles.
SNOWFLAKE MAP LOCATOR #126

PRESCOTT

America's Attic
235 N. Pleasant St., Prescott, AZ 86301
445-0212   Open Tu-Sa 11-5
Silver, glass, china, light fixtures, art, furniture, etc.
PRESCOTT MAP LOCATOR #127

Antiques & Originals-Leo & Lori Scott, Owners
140 N. Cortez St., Prescott, AZ 86301
Turn N off Gurley St; located on W side of street.
778-6006 or 445-9335   Open M-F 10-4
Furniture, collectibles, glass, silver, radios, phonographs, etc.
PRESCOTT MAP LOCATOR #128

Arizona Territory Antiques-Herb & Lila Cook, Owners
211 W. Aubrey St., Prescott, AZ 86301
445-4656   Open W-Sa 9:30-5
General line.
PRESCOTT MAP LOCATOR #129

PRESCOTT (cont.)

Carriage House Antiques
211 E. Willis St., Prescott, AZ 86301
Behind yellow Victorian house at the corner of Marina and Willis.
778-6323   Open Tu-Sa 11-5, Su by appt.
Full of country pine and oak furniture primitives, glassware, pottery and unique kitchen collectibles.
PRESCOTT MAP LOCATOR #130

Drake Depot Antiques
1533 Iron Springs Rd., Prescott, AZ 86301
774-4380   Open Tu-Su 10-5
Antiques and collectibles; furniture for home and office, quilts, linens, etc.
PRESCOTT MAP LOCATOR #131

East to West Antiques
142 S. Montezuma St., Prescott, AZ 86301
On Whiskey Row.
445-4354   Open M-Sa 10-5:30
Fine line of antiques direct from the East coast.
PRESCOTT MAP LOCATOR #132

Fran's Antiques-Fran Mahoney, Owner
346 S. Montezuma St., Prescott, AZ 86301
3 blks S of historical Whiskey Row.
445-0314   Open daily 10:30-5
Clocks, furniture, china, collectibles. Buy, sell and consign. Located in old restored Victorian home.
PRESCOTT MAP LOCATOR #133

Granite Dells Rock Shop
Rt. 5, Box 915, Prescott, AZ 86301
At the Jct. of 89 & 89A.
445-5350   Open Tu-Su 9-5
Collectibles, some furniture and glass.

Hartin's Red Door Antiques
140 N. Cortez St., Prescott, AZ 86301
445-4691   Open daily, please ring bell.
Fine dolls and early American primitives.
PRESCOTT MAP LOCATOR #134

PRESCOTT (cont.)

The Heritage Shoppe-Alice M. Tope, Owner
723 E. Gurley St., Prescott, AZ   86301
445-8706   Open Tu-Sa 9:30-4:30
A variety of items; browsers welcome and buyers adored.
PRESCOTT MAP LOCATOR #135

J & J Antiques
1606 Kile St., Prescott, AZ   86301
778-9053   Open M-Sa 10-5 and by appt.
Large selection of fine oak furniture. Also, glassware and primitives.
Specializing in custom furniture restoration.
PRESCOTT MAP LOCATOR #136

Joy's Antiques
1870 Meadowridge Rd., Prescott, AZ   86301
445-3463   Open by appt. only.
Furniture and lamp painting. Also, large selection of glassware, china and
primitives.
PRESCOTT MAP LOCATOR #137

Karen Antiques
442 S. Montezuma St., Prescott, AZ   86301
778-1510 or 778-1741   Open W-Sa 11-4
Victorian jewelry, country primitives, majolica, brass, silver and glass.
PRESCOTT MAP LOCATOR #138

Liese Interiors & Artifacts
140 S. Montezuma, Prescott, AZ   86301
445-2431   Open M-Sa 9-5
Antique jewelry and beads.
PRESCOTT MAP LOCATOR #139

Margaret Lambert Antiques & Accessories
342 S. Montezuma St., B, Prescott, AZ   86301
Open W-Sa 10-4
PRESCOTT MAP LOCATOR #140

PRESCOTT (cont.)

Prescott Antique & Craft Market-Steve & Barbara Hire, Owners
115 N. Cortez St., Prescott, AZ 86301
W on Gurley to downtown Courthouse Square; turn rt. on Cortez.
445-7156   Open M-Sa 10-5, Su 12-5
60 shops, 6000 sq. ft., 2 stories, furniture, collectibles, vintage clothing, glass, pottery, coins, rare books, etc. *See ad on back cover.*
PRESCOTT MAP LOCATOR #141

Sally Ann's Collectibles
232 N. Granite St., P.O. Box 590, Prescott, AZ 86301
778-4660   Open W-Sa 11-6
Large rooms filled with fine English furniture, glassware, pottery, jewelry and nice accessories for the home.
PRESCOTT MAP LOCATOR #142

Two Beaks Antiques
1602 Adams St., Prescott, AZ 86301
445-4448   Open Tu-Sa 10-5
Large stock of wicker, old harness, tack and old tools.

Whiskey Row Emporium-D. Templin Walker & Jerolyn Miner, Owners
110 Whiskey Row, Prescott, AZ 86301
778-3091   Open M-Sa 10-5, Su 11-4
Over 30 dealers featuring antiques and collectibles.
PRESCOTT MAP LOCATOR #143

RIVIERA (See Bullhead City)

SCOTTSDALE

Antiques & Precious Things
7125 E. Main St., Scottsdale, AZ 85251
947-4621   Open M-Sa 12-4, Closed July-September.
Victorian jewelry and small glasswares, china and crystal. *See ad on page 65.*
SCOTTSDALE MAP LOCATOR #144

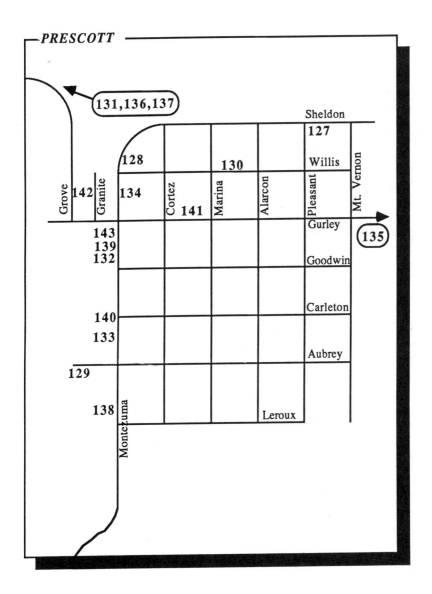

SCOTTSDALE (cont.)

Arden Gallery-Patrick Payne, Ilona Gibbs & Michael Chesworth, Owners
7019 E. Main St., Scottsdale, AZ   85251
Between Marshall Way and 70th St.
990-9101   Open M-Sa 10-5
American branch of English firm established in 1965 specializing in imported antique and contemporary European oil paintings and frames.
SCOTTSDALE MAP LOCATOR #145

Arizona West Galleries, Inc.-A.P. Hays, Owner
7161 Main St., Scottsdale, AZ   85251
Half blk W of Scottsdale Rd. on Main.
994-3752   Open M-Sa 10-5, Summers by appt. only.
Old West collector's gallery; paintings, drawings, bronzes by Western Masters, Remington, Russell, James, cowboy and military relics.
SCOTTSDALE MAP LOCATOR #146

Benner & Co. Antiques-Carolyn Benner, Owner
947-9260   Open by appt. only.
See ad on page 67.

Bette Lou Mulligan Antiques-Bette Lou Mulligan, Owner
7077 Main St., Scottsdale, AZ   85251
994-4390   Open M-Sa 11-5 except Summer.
Jewelry, silver and country furnishings. *See ad on page 67.*
SCOTTSDALE MAP LOCATOR #147

Bishop Gallery-W. P. Bishop, Owner
7164 Main St., Scottsdale, AZ   85251
949-9062   Open M-Sa 10-5, Tu 7PM-10PM
Folk art from around the world. African and New Guinea art. Oriental antiques.
SCOTTSDALE MAP LOCATOR #148

Brown House II Antiques-Esther Lynn Johnson, Owner
7116 Main St., Scottsdale, AZ 85251
W of Scottsdale Rd.
994-4318   Open M-Sa 10-5
American period and country furniture. Quilts, dolls and toys. *See ad on page 69.*
SCOTTSDALE MAP LOCATOR #149

The Clock Doctor
7144 E. Stetson Dr., Scottsdale, AZ 85251
1 blk S of Camelback and 1 blk W of Scottsdale Rd.
994-3104   Open M-F 10-5, Sa 10-3
Expert repair of watches and clocks.
SCOTTSDALE MAP LOCATOR #150

Curiosity Shoppe, Ltd.-M. Michaels, Owner
7300 E. Stetson Dr., Scottsdale, AZ 85251
941-3777   Open Tu-Sa 10:30-4
Fine antiques and accessories.
SCOTTSDALE MAP LOCATOR #151

David Adler Antiques-David Adler, Owner
7039 Main St., Scottsdale, AZ 85251
941-2995   Open M-Sa 10-5
Antiques and oriental rugs.
SCOTTSDALE MAP LOCATOR #152

The Doll House-Lillian Zang, Manager
6107 N. Scottsdale Rd., Scottsdale, AZ 85253
In the Hilton Village Center.
948-4630   Open M-Sa 10-5:30
Antique dolls and miniatures.
SCOTTSDALE MAP LOCATOR #153

Golden West Galleries-Barney Goldberg, Owner
7130 Main St., Scottsdale, AZ 85251
On Main St. between Scottsdale Rd. and Marshall Way.
941-5164   Open M-Sa 10-5
Featuring the finest in 19th and 20th century American and Southwestern art as well as sculpture for the discriminating collector.
SCOTTSDALE MAP LOCATOR #154

SCOTTSDALE (cont.)

Hob Nobbin'-Martha Reding, Owner
7120 E. Indian School Rd., Scottsdale, AZ 85251
N side of the street just W of Scottsdale Rd.
949-9090   Open M-Sa 10-5
Lovely old linens, jewelry, art glass, Haviland, oriental items and furniture.
SCOTTSDALE MAP LOCATOR #155

Impeccable Pig
7042 E. Indian School Rd., Scottsdale, AZ 85251
2 blks W of Scottsdale Rd.
941-1141   Open M-Sa 9AM-10PM
American and primitive antiques.
SCOTTSDALE MAP LOCATOR #156

J. H. Armer, Co.-J. H. Armer, Owner
6926 Main St., Scottsdale, AZ 85251
947-2407   Open M-Sa 9-5
English, country furniture and accessories.
SCOTTSDALE MAP LOCATOR #157

Joan's Antiques
6934 5th Ave., Suite 101A, Scottsdale, AZ 85251
949-1041   Open Tu-Sa 12-5
English, oriental porcelain, antique jewelry, sterling and fine crystal.
SCOTTSDALE MAP LOCATOR #158

M & B Unlimited
7502 E. Monterey Way, Scottsdale, AZ 85251
990-1757
SCOTTSDALE MAP LOCATOR #159

Main Street Antiques-Susan Peevyhouse, Owner
7077 E. Main St., Suite 2, Scottsdale, AZ 85251
945-8591   Open M-Sa 11-5
A general line including antique jewelry, period furniture, Americana,
nouveau/deco, quilts, samplers, sterling and majolica. *See ad on page 67.*
MAP LOCATOR #160

1855 FRIENDSHIP QUILT

BROWN HOUSE ANTIQUES

A Wide Variety of Fine Antiques
ANTIQUE DOLLS & TOYS A SPECIALTY

7116 Main St.
Scottsdale, AZ
994-4318

SCOTTSDALE (cont.)

Marsha's Fifth Avenue Scottsdale
7121 5th Ave., Scottsdale, AZ 85251
SE corner of 5th Ave. and Craftsman Court.
946-0141   Open M-Sa 10-5
Oriental only.
SCOTTSDALE MAP LOCATOR #161

Mistinguett Gallery
7133 E. Main St., Scottsdale, AZ 85251
947-4434   Open M-Sa 11-5:30, Su by appt.
French provincial antiques (1900-1930).
SCOTTSDALE MAP LOCATOR #162

Morris Antiques
7077 E. Main St., Scottsdale, AZ 85251
949-1016   Open M-Sa 10-5
China, cut glass, silver and jewelry. *See ad on page 71.*
SCOTTSDALE MAP LOCATOR #163

Neighbor Lady's Antiques
7014 1st Ave., Scottsdale, AZ 85251
947-6663   Open M-Sa 11-5
Specializing in American furniture, accessories, quilts, folk art and majolica.
SCOTTSDALE MAP LOCATOR #164

Past Times Antiques & Collectibles-Brenda J. Patterson, Owner
7236 E. 1st Ave., Scottsdale, AZ 85251
1 blk S of Indian School Rd.; E of Scottsdale Rd.
990-7675   Open M-Sa 11-4, Su 1-4
Featuring fine china, glass, silver, jewelry, antique and collectible dolls, quilts, clocks, furniture, old prints and maps.
SCOTTSDALE MAP LOCATOR #165

Pine Interiors-Ilona Johnson-Gibbs & Patrick Payne, Owners
7019 E. Main St., Scottsdale, AZ 85251
Between Marshall Way and 70th St.
941-8798   Open M-Sa 10-5
The largest importers of antique country pine furniture in the SW with monthly containers from Europe.
SCOTTSDALE MAP LOCATOR #166

ANTIQUE FIX-UP TIPS...

Your antiques can be kept looking their best by utilizing many of these cleaning tips!

BRASS
To polish brass, apply worcestershire sauce to the surface, scrub with an SOS pad, rinse and wipe dry.

COPPER
Polish your copper by pouring ketchup onto the surface, then scrub with an SOS pad.

FURNITURE
Scratches on wood furniture will disappear by using the meat from a walnut and rubbing it into the scratch. Other remedies include a matching color of eyebrow pencil or a permanent marking pen.

Water rings can be rubbed out with Mentholatum or mayonnaise. Let set for 8 hours, then lightly sand with a dry Scotch-Brite pad and polish with oil.

Wood items that need refurbishing but don't need to be stripped should receive a coat of lacquer thinner, then buffed with "4-0" steel wool. This cleans the wood and prepares it for staining or oiling.

Lemon oil on wood returns some of the natural oils and helps to prevent the wood from drying out.

METAL
Lemon oil is good to restore metals and returns their luster after they have been cleaned.

WASHBOARDS
When restoring a washboard, clean the metal portion with a high quality metal cleaner. Use lacquer thinner and "4-0" steel wool to clean the wood parts. Boiled linseed oil will restore the wood.

SCOTTSDALE (cont.)

Pueblo One
3815 N. Brown Ave., Scottdale , AZ 85251
1 blk E of Scottsdale Rd., 3 blk S of Indian School.
946-7271   Open M-F 9:30-4:30, Sa 10-2
Antique American, Indian art and Spanish colonial items.
SCOTTDALE MAP LOCATOR #167

Rails West, Ltd.
7303 E. Indian Bend Rd., Scottsdale, AZ 85253
In McCormick Railroad Park, corner of Scottsdale and Indian Bend Rds.
991-3995   Open W-Su 10-5
Railroad related antiques, artifacts, books, etc. Located in railroad theme park.
SCOTTSDALE MAP LOCATOR #168

Rose Tree Antiques
10634 N. 71st Pl., Scottsdale, AZ 85254
In Sundown Plaza.
948-5263   Open M-W, F-Sa 11-5
Antique and collectible American and European furniture, china, crystal, brass,
bronze, silver, orientalia and fine art.
SCOTTSDALE MAP LOCATOR #169

Scottsdale Floweranch-Barbara Goldie, Owner
3202 N. Scottsdale Rd., Scottsdale, AZ 85251
S of Osborn on W side of Scottsdale Rd.
990-7775   Open M-F 8-6, Sa 8-4
Small American and English antiques.
SCOTTSDALE MAP LOCATOR #170

Silver Spring Emporium-Barbara Nicks, Owner
4017 N. 69th St., Scottsdale, AZ 85251
941-0272   Closed Summers.
SCOTTSDALE MAP LOCATOR #171

Sweetest Charity
3704 N. Scottsdale Rd., Scottsdale, AZ 85251
Between Indian School and Osborn
941-2969   Open M-Sa 10-6, Su 12-5
Large selection of Victoriana through 50's clothing; hats, bags, shoes, jewelry
for men, women, kids. Rentals, too.
SCOTTSDALE MAP LOCATOR #172

SCOTTSDALE (cont.)

Ye Olde Curiosity Shoppe
7245 1st Ave., Scottsdale, AZ 85251
1 blk S of Indian School, E of Scottsdale Rd.
947-3062   Open M-Sa 11-5, Closed Mondays June-August
Dolls, clothing and jewelry.
SCOTTSDALE MAP LOCATOR #173

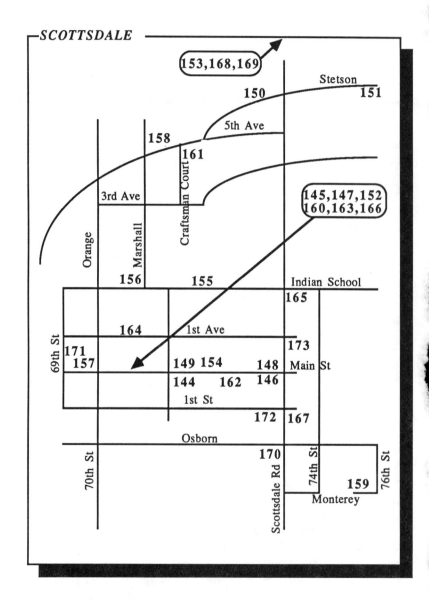

SEDONA

Antiquity Shoppe-Beverly Goss, Owner
1670 W. Hwy 89A, Sedona, AZ 86336
282-2266   Open M-Sa 10-5
Oak furniture, Depression glass and caning. *See ad on page 77.*

Delightful Muddle Antiques
Hwy 179 & 89A, Sedona, AZ 86336
At the "Y."
282-4343   Open daily 11-4

Designed Interiors
2550 W. 89A, Sedona, AZ 86336
Smith's corner.
282-9757   Open M-F 10-5, Sa 10-2
Antiques and antique reproductions.

Esteban Pottery & Antiques
Hwy 179, Sedona, AZ 86336
In the Tlaquepaque Shopping Center.
282-4686   Open M-Sa 10-5, Su 11-5
Pottery plus oak, walnut and Victorian furniture.

Unique Furniture & Antiques-Vi Shirley, Owner
3004 Hwy 89A, Sedona, AZ 86336
Turn W at Int. 79A and 89A; 2 1/2 miles down on 89A.
282-2221 or 282-9402   Open M-Sa 10:30-5, Su by appt.
Art glass, china, silver, furniture, lamps, mirrors, local art, lampshades, jewelry, gift items and more! *See ad on page 77.*

SHOW LOW

Cheryl's Antiques & Indian Artifacts
1100 E. Deuce of Clubs, Show Low, AZ 85901
On Main St. down in the basement.
537-4246   Open M-Sa 9-5
Indian artifacts.
SNOWFLAKE MAP LOCATOR #174

SKULL VALLEY

Skull Valley Store
30 minutes from Prescott.
442-3351   Open M-Sa 7-5:30
Quaint old country store setting with selection of antique furniture, glassware, knick knacks and collectibles.

SNOWFLAKE

The Country Cupboard-Tina Baldwin, Owner
Star Rt. 1, Snowflake, AZ   85937
536-2273
Gifts, antiques, collectibles, home and country accessories.
SNOWFLAKE MAP LOCATOR #175

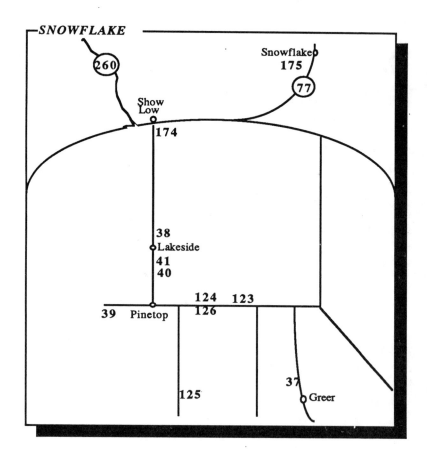

SUN CITY

Fritz' Coins & Antiques
11001 99th Ave., Sun City, AZ 85351
933-5373   Open M-Sa 9-5
Coins and antiques.

TEMPE

Antique International Marketplace-Marilyn Carey, Manager
1815 E. Apache Blvd., Tempe, AZ 85281
SE corner or Apache and McClintock.
968-5053   Open Tu-Sa 10-6, Su 12-6, Th 10-8
Arizona's largest air-conditioned marketplace of antiques, collectibles, arts and crafts selected from around the world. 30 dealers! *See ad on page 79.*
TEMPE MAP LOCATOR #176

Antique Radio & Tube Co.
1725 W. University, Tempe, AZ   85281
On S side of University E of 52nd St.
894-9503   Open M-F 9-5, Sa 9-1
Antique radios and related items.
TEMPE MAP LOCATOR #177

Dyana's
622 S. Mill Ave., Tempe, AZ   85281
1 blk N of University at 7th St.
966-2844   Open M-Sa 10-6
Vintage clothing and costume rental.
TEMPE MAP LOCATOR #178

Jim's Jukebox Warehouse
910 S. Hohokam, Suite 120, Tempe, AZ   85281
894-2656   Open by appt. only.
Antique jukeboxes, slot machines, gumball machines, parts, service and rental.
TEMPE MAP LOCATOR #179

Maranatha Antiques
904 N. Scottsdale Rd., Tempe, AZ   85281
W side of Scottsdale at Curry.
966-1562   Open M-Sa 10-6, Su 1-6
Largest selection of oak in town.
TEMPE MAP LOCATOR #180

Scottsdale Auction & Antiques, Inc.-Pam Johnston, Lee Johnston &
Jim Bertone, Owners
2150A W. University Drive, Tempe, AZ   85281
W University near 44th St.
894-0071   Open M-Sa 10-6
American, European furniture. Unusual American pieces and some
reproductions. Contact for bi-monthly auction information.
TEMPE MAP LOCATOR #181

Antique International Marketplace

Arizona's largest, Air Conditioned marketplace
of Antiques and Collectables, Arts and Crafts
selected around the world.

Over 30 dealer shops offer increased selection and services.

Tues.-Sat. 10-6
Sun. 12-6
Thursday 10-8

Buy/Sell/Trade - Layaways

1815 E. Apache
Tempe, AZ 85281

(602) 968-5053

South East corner of Apache and McClintock

TEMPE (cont.)

Those Were the Days!
516 S. Mill Ave., Tempe, AZ   85281
I-10 to 44th St., N exit, N to University, E to Mill, then N.
967-4729   Open M-F 9:30-6, Th 9:30-9, Sa 10:30-5:30, Su 12-5
Refinished Victorian oak, walnut furniture, advertising, over 1000 titles of new books about antiques and collectibles. *See ad on page 81.*
TEMPE MAP LOCATOR #182

Traders Den Antiques
1006 W. University Dr., Tempe, AZ   85281
N side of University at Hardy.
966-8322   Open M, T, Th-Sa 10-5
TEMPE MAP LOCATOR #183

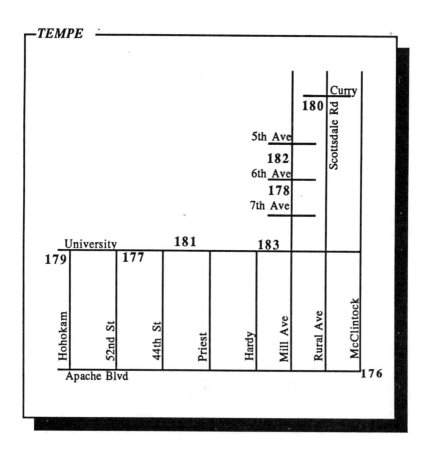

THATCHER

Antiques of Distinction-Joe & Gwen Ceccardi, Owners ·
702 Main, Thatcher, AZ 85552
Corner of Hwy 70 and Stadium Ave. in Thatcher.
428-1503   Open Tu-Sa 9-5 and by appt.
Predominantly elegant antique furniture; collectibles and glassware, oak
reproductions at competitive prices. Strip and refinishing.

TOMBSTONE

Rose Tree Inn-Burton Devere, Owner
116 S. 4th, Tombstone, AZ 85638
In the city limits, corner of 4th and Toughnut.
457-3326   Open M-Su 9-5
Old Wedgewood, Blackmark, Irish Belleek, English porcelain, glass and
primitives. General line, no furniture.

WEST TUCSON

Mission Antiques-Shirley Mailloux & Ed Rahbe, Owners
Milepost 152, Tucson, AZ 85735
822-1020
Fine old lamps, early lighting fixtures, oak furniture and a myriad of interesting
accessories. Furniture repair and refinishing.
WEST TUCSON MAP LOCATOR #184

DOWNTOWN TUCSON

America West Primitive Arts-Kelley Rollings, Owner
363 S. Meyer Ave., Tucson, AZ 85701
Half blk S of Tucson Community Center.
623-4091   Open M-Sa 10-4 and by appt.
American Indian, Americana, pre-Columbian, African, Oceanic, oriental and
ancient arts. Emphasis on sculpture, paintings, etc.
DOWNTOWN TUCSON MAP LOCATOR #185

Barbara Skilton Appraising & Consulting
666 W. Rillito Ln., Tucson, AZ 85705
887-2140   Open by appt. only.
China, jewelry, fine glass and vintage clothing.

Elegant Junque Shop-Tina & Wayne Olson, Owners
2828 N. Stone Ave., Tucson, AZ 85705
622-8773   Open M-Sa 10-5:30
One of the most interesting shops in the state; a fabulous clutter of wonderful
old things, advertising, furniture and Hummels. *See ad on page 83.*
DOWNTOWN TUCSON MAP LOCATOR #186

Gibson Antiques-Johnny & Pearle Gibson, Owners
39 N. 6th Ave., Tucson, AZ 85701
Downtown Tucson between Congress & Pennington.
623-9037   Open M-Sa 9-5
Fine wood furniture, barber chairs, paintings, dressers, buffets. Rentals to
movies, stage plays, etc.
DOWNTOWN TUCSON MAP LOCATOR #187

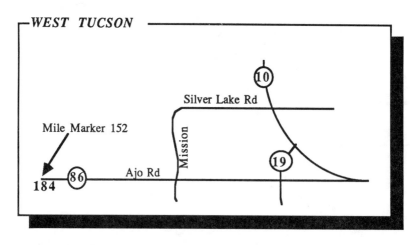

Glastiques & Things-Steve & Marty Dix, Owners
337 E. Grant Rd., Tucson, AZ 85705
Between 1st and Stone Aves., on N side of Grant.
623-7776   Open M-Th, Sa 10-5, Closed Summers
Art glass, china and crytstal, prints, lithographs, etchings, oil paintings,
watercolors, furniture, primitives, folk art, etc.
DOWNTOWN TUCSON MAP LOCATOR #188

How Sweet It Was Vintage Clothing-Connie & Kathleen Lauth,
Owners
636 N. 4th Ave., Tucson, AZ 85705
623-9854   Open M-F 11-6, Sa 10-6
Vintage clothing, costumes and rentals.
DOWNTOWN TUCSON MAP LOCATOR #189

Lastenia's Antiques
2550 N. Stone Ave., Tucson, AZ 85705
622-7882   Open Tu-Sa 9:30-5:30
General line.
DOWNTOWN TUCSON MAP LOCATOR #190

Nettie's Treasures
135 E. Congress St., Tucson, AZ 85701
622-6382
Vintage clothing, jewelry, Depression glass, ceramics and crystal.
DOWNTOWN TUCSON MAP LOCATOR #191

DOWNTOWN TUCSON (cont.)

Nova Glass Works, Inc.
1448 N. Stone Ave., Tucson, AZ 85705
1 blk W of Drachman on the SE corner or Stone & Adams.
622-6955   Open M-Sa 9-5:30
Repairs, restorations, lamps, window, Becker stained glass gallery. Bent glass
lamp repair a specialty.
DOWNTOWN TUCSON MAP LOCATOR #192

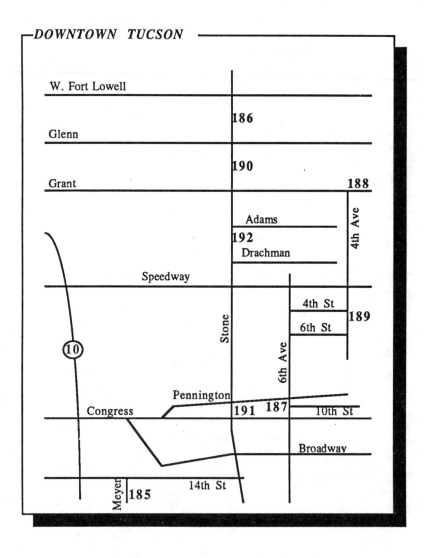

DOWNTOWN TUCSON

CENTRAL TUCSON

Antique Mini-Mall-Julian & Ruth Blakely, Owners
3408 E. Grant Rd., Tucson, AZ 85716
336-6502   Open M-Sa 10-5:30, Su 1-5
14 dealers featuring a general line. *See ad below.*
CENTRAL TUCSON MAP LOCATOR #193

The Antique Traveler
36 N. Tucson Blvd., Tucson, AZ 85716
325-3050

Associated Appraisers-Betty L. Berry, Owner
2627 E. Broadway Blvd., Tucson, AZ 85716
Between Country Club and Tucson Blvd.
795-1312   Open Tu-F 9:30-4:30, Sa 9:30-2:30
Appraisals and insuranced estates.
CENTRAL TUCSON MAP LOCATOR #194

The Broadway Gallery-Betty L. Berry, Owner
2627 E. Broadway Blvd., Tucson, AZ 85716
Between Country Club & Tucson Blvd.
323-0967   Open Tu-F 9:30-4:30, Sa 9:30-2:30
Period furniture, porcelain and glass, Georgian silver, oriental, Americana,
Western art, bronzes and oriental rugs.
CENTRAL TUCSON MAP LOCATOR #194

Country Emporium Antiques-Mr. & Mrs. T. F. Walker, Owners
3431 N. Dodge Blvd., Tucson, AZ 85716
Take Grant Rd. exit off I-10 E to Dodge Blvd., turn N on Dodge.
327-7765   Open M-Sa 10-5
Southwest Americana; country and oak furniture, advertising, country and
kitchen items, Western and mining relics, and collectibles. *See ad on page 87.*
CENTRAL TUCSON MAP LOCATOR #195

Country Trading Post
2815 N. Country Club Rd., Tucson, AZ 85716
325-7326   Open M-Su 9-5
General line, restoration.
CENTRAL TUCSON MAP LOCATOR #196

Eisenhut Antiques-Dick & Marcia Eisenhut, Owners
2313 N. Country Club Rd., Tucson, AZ 85716
Country Club at Grant.
325-5685   Open Tu-Sa 9-5, Su 12-3
American furniture, primitives, antique lighting, fine glass and pottery.
CENTRAL TUCSON MAP LOCATOR #197

Just Us American Antiques
622-3607   Open by appt. only.
General line including quilts.

Phyliss' Antiques & Indian Jewelry
1918 E. Prince Rd., Tucson, AZ 85719
326-5712   Open Tu-Sa 12-5 and by appt.
Indian jewelry, oriental and costume jewelry plus dishes.
CENTRAL TUCSON MAP LOCATOR #198

Primitive Arts-Michael Higgins & Paul S. Shepard, Owners
3026 E. Broadway Blvd., Tucson, AZ 85716
Broadway at Country Club.
326-4852   Open Tu-Sa 10-4
American Indian, pre-Columbian and American folk art.
CENTRAL TUCSON MAP LOCATOR #199

Rural America Antiques-Don Wood, Owner
2818 N. Country Club Rd., Tucson, AZ 85716
Just N of Glenn.
326-0889   Open M-Sa 9-5
Oak, pine, other fine wood furniture. Kitchen collectibles, landscaping
collectibles, mirrors, Minwax-Deft distributor. Mirror resilvering and
reproduction hardware. *See ad on page 89.*
CENTRAL TUCSON MAP LOCATOR #200

CENTRAL TUCSON (cont.)

The Sports Page-Mike McDonald, Mgr.
1680 N. Country Club Rd., Tucson, AZ 85716
SE corner of Pima & Country Club.
326-5001 Open M-F 11-5:30, Sa 10-5
Baseball cards, other sports collectibles, sports books, souvenirs, etc.
CENTRAL TUCSON MAP LOCATOR #201

Sunland Antiques, Inc.-Sid & Pat Leluan, Owners
2206-2208 N. Country Club Rd., Tucson, AZ 85716
323-1134 Open M-Sa 9-5
English imports.
CENTRAL TUCSON MAP LOCATOR #202

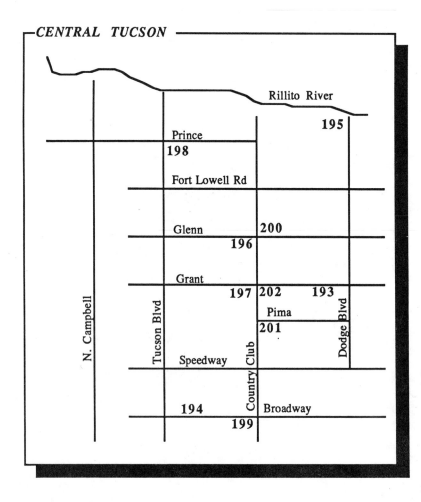

EAST TUCSON

A & A Antiques
8677 E. Golf Links Rd., Tucson, AZ 85730
886-8153   Open M-Sa 8:30-6, Su 10:30-6
American primitive antiques and collectibles.
EAST TUCSON MAP LOCATOR #203

Accent Antiques
908 N. Swan Rd., Tucson, AZ 85711
326-3505   Open M-Sa 10-5:30, Su 1-5
Oriental and Victorian antiques, unusual things.
EAST TUCSON MAP LOCATOR #204

Antique Clock Mart
5665 E. 22nd St., Tucson, AZ 85710
747-5674   Open Tu-Sa 10-5
Fine antique clocks; sold, repaired, bought and appraised.
EAST TUCSON MAP LOCATOR #205

Antique Jewelry Exchange
4730 E. Speedway Blvd., Tucson, AZ 85712
E on Speedway past Swan, 3 doors from corner on S side of street.
881-6525   Open M-Sa 10-5
Antique and estate jewelry, Victorian, filigree, deco and contemporary jewelry.
Diamonds and diamond jewelry at unbeatable prices.
EAST TUCSON MAP LOCATOR #206

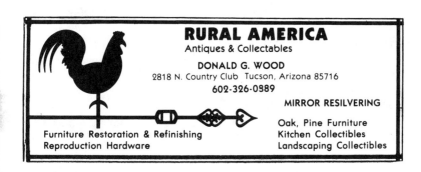

Barkley Appraisals
802 N. Irving Circle, Tucson, AZ 85711
323-2222   Open by appt. only.
Appraisals only.
EAST TUCSON MAP LOCATOR #207

Cards, Etc.
5629 E. 22nd St., Tucson, AZ 85711
748-2747   Open M-Sa 10-5
Sports collectibles, baseball cards, yearbooks, uniform items 1900-present.
EAST TUCSON MAP LOCATOR #208

Christine's Curiosity Shop & Doll Museum
4940 E. Speedway Blvd., Tucson, AZ 85712
Between Swan and Craycroft on Speedway.
323-0018   Open M-Sa 10-5:30
Dolls, Victorian furniture, glass, silver and appraising.
EAST TUCSON MAP LOCATOR #209

Far Horizons
4659 E. North St., Tucson, AZ 85712
325-7072   Open W-Sa 10-5, Su 12-5 (May to August) and by appt.
Period furniture, silver, porcelain, art glass and cut glass.
EAST TUCSON MAP LOCATOR #210

Firehouse Antiques & Gifts-Leslee Lillywhite, Manager.
7810 Tanque Verde Rd., Tucson, AZ 85715
The old Rural Metro.
721-0659   Open W-Sa 10-5, Su 12-5
European, primitives, rolltop desks, artifacts. Will search out requests! *See ad on page 91.*
EAST TUCSON MAP LOCATOR #211

Fretwork Antiques-Terry & Dean, Owners
4545 E. Broadway Blvd., Tucson, AZ 85711
327-9400   Open Tu-Sa 9-5:30
Golden oak furniture and leaded windows.
EAST TUCSON MAP LOCATOR #212

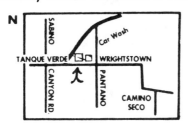

Golden Eagle Antiques & Appraising-Jack Jackson & Ginger Jackson
Carter, Owners
5917 E. 3rd St., Tucson, AZ 85711
790-3333   Open by appt. only
EAST TUCSON MAP LOCATOR #213

J. R.'s Antiques
4223 E. Grant Rd., Tucson, AZ 85712
325-1037   Open M-Sa 10-5
Oak, pine, walnut furniture. Primitives, pottery and glassware.
EAST TUCSON MAP LOCATOR #214

Kay Mallex
3859 E. Grant Rd., Tucson, AZ 85712
326-1642   Open M-Sa 9-6
Period furniture, paintings, prints, quilts, coverlets, samplers, stitchery,
orientalia, ivory scrimshaw, oriental rugs, etc.
EAST TUCSON MAP LOCATOR #215

Lucy's Loft
2936 E. Grant Rd., Tucson, AZ 85716
795-0432   Open Tu-Sa 9-5
Glass, china, collectibles and vintage clothing.

Old & Green
3955 E. Broadway Blvd., Tucson, AZ 85711
323-9116   Open M-Sa 10:30-5
Furniture and collectibles.
EAST TUCSON MAP LOCATOR #216

Sandy's Antiques & Jewelry-Sandy Grossman, Owner
3950 E. Speedway Blvd., Tucson, AZ 85712
327-0772
Costume and fine jewelry, furniture, dolls, crystal, antiques and collectibles.
EAST TUCSON MAP LOCATOR #217

Up Home Country Shop-Leigh Gault, Owner
3950 E. Speedway Blvd., Tucson, AZ 85712
327-0772
Antiques, collectibles, crafts, furniture, gifts and toys.
EAST TUCSON MAP LOCATOR #217

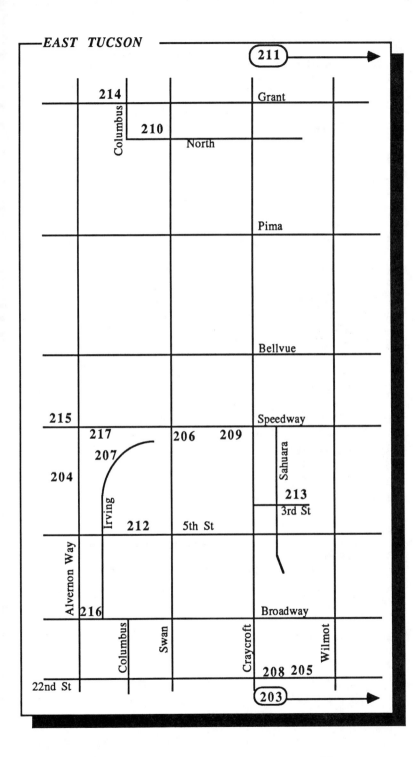

EAST TUCSON

211

214

Columbus

210

Grant

North

Pima

Bellvue

215

Speedway

217 206 209

207

Sahuara

204

213

3rd St

Irving

212 5th St

Alvernon Way

216

Broadway

Columbus

Swan

Craycroft

Wilmot

22nd St

208 205

203

WICKENBURG

Den of Antiquity-Dani Garrity, Owner
681 Whipple, Wickenburg, AZ 85358
On California Hwy. next to the Western Deli.
684-5986   Open M-Sa 9-5
Depression glass, oriental and collectibles.

Memories & More-Lela M. Shipley, Owner
692 Whipple, Wickenburg, AZ 85358
5 1/2 blks W of intersection on Rt. 60.
684-3287   Open M-Sa 10-5
Quality pieces including pattern glass, cut glass, Haviland, old fostoria,
Depression, antique jewelry, buttons, thimbles, etc.

WILLCOX

Rocking Chair Antiques-Gordon & Anne Stoddard, Owners
Rt. 1, Box 814, Willcox, AZ 85643
3 miles N of Willcox on Fort Grant Rd.
384-4338   Open by appt. only.
A variety of antiques and collectibles.

WINSLOW

Country Peddlers-Ann, June, Ruth & Jeannie, Owners
318 W. 3rd St., Winslow, AZ 86047
1 way through center of town; obtainable by all 3 freeway exits.
289-5446   Open Tu-Sa 10-5
Antiques, Depression glass, soft-sculptured dolls, unique crafts, decorating ideas
for country living. An ideal gift shop.

YARNELL

Things Remembered
162 Broadway, Yarnell, AZ 85362
427-3515   Open M-W, F-Su 10-5
Fine quality porcelain and glass.

YARNELL (cont.)

Yarnell Bits & Pieces-Ernie & Ginny Padrutt, Owners
193 Broadway, Yarnell, AZ 85362
427-3174
Antiques, collectibles and gifts.

YOUNGTOWN

Julia's Antiques
11122 W. Alabama Ave., Youngtown, AZ 85363
972-8673   Open M-F 10-4
Something for everyone.

YUMA

Ave. B Furniture
2910 Ave. B, Yuma, AZ 85364
726-5053   Open M-Sa 9-5
Furniture, miscellaneous antiques and collectibles.
YUMA MAP LOCATOR #218

The Bargain Spot
385 S. Main St., Yuma, AZ 85364
783-5889   Open M-Sa 10-4
General line.
YUMA MAP LOCATOR #219

Gila Gallery Antiques
195 S. Gila St., Yuma, AZ 85364
783-6128   Open Tu-Sa 10-4:30 or by appt.
American and English furniture, plus some collectibles.
YUMA MAP LOCATOR #220

Olde Town Antiques
381 S. Main St., Yuma, AZ 85364
782-5284   Open Tu-Sa 10-4:30
Collectibles, art, glass and furniture.
YUMA MAP LOCATOR #221

Potpourri
720 3rd St., Yuma, AZ
For the unusual in antiques, clothing and collectibles.
YUMA MAP LOCATOR #222

YUMA (cont.)

Sherman's Antiques & Collectibles-Wayne & Billie Sherman, Owners
1250 S. 3rd Ave., Yuma, AZ 85364
From I-8 take 16th St. exit to 4th Ave., turn rt to 13th St.
783-8913   Open M-F 12-5, Sa by chance
Turn-of-the-century oak furniture.
YUMA MAP LOCATOR #223

Westward Village Shops-D. H. Trigg, Owner
3300 S. 8th Ave., Yuma, AZ 85365
Turn S from 32nd St. on 8th Ave. Go one blk on gravel road.
726-1417   Open Tu-Su 10-5 (except Summer)
YUMA MAP LOCATOR #224

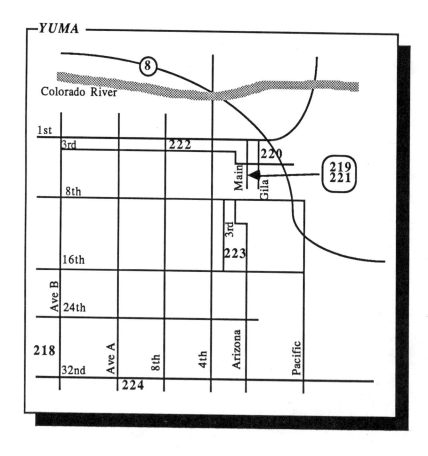

INDEX-Services

The following businesses specialize in these **ANTIQUE** services:

INDEX-Specialties

The following businesses specialize in these items:

INDEX-Specialties (cont.)

ANTIQUE SHOW PROMOTERS...

Acorn Antique Guild-Larry & Nedra Quick
P.O. Box 2337, Mesa, AZ 85204
962-5503
See ad on page 101.

Arizona Depression Glass Club-Howard Bertsch & Barbara Chase
247-8207 (Howard) or 956-2829 (Barbara)
See ad on page 101.

Arizona Toy Round Up-V. Koenke
904 E. San Juan, Phoenix, AZ 85014
274-7423

Bustamante Enterprises, Inc.
P.O. Box 637, Atwater, CA 95301-0637
(209) 358-3134

Gold Rush Shows-Frances Poage
22831 N. 83rd Ave., Peoria, AZ 85345
974-0967

Goodwill Antique Sale
417 N. 16th St., Phoenix, AZ 85006
254-2222 or 258-7046

Jerome Chamber of Commerce-Dennis Mead
P.O. Box 788, Jerome, AZ 86331
634-5716
See ad on page 101.

Phoenix Art Museum-Joan Palmer & Pam Grandquist
252-9422 (Joan) or 257-1880 (Pam)

Southwest Antique Guild-Marvin & Marian Little
P.O. Box 3535, West Sedona, AZ 86340
282-3153
See ad on page 103.

Sunland Antiques, Inc.-Sid Leluan
206 N. Country Club Dr., Tucson, AZ 85716
323-1134

ANTIQUE SHOW PROMOTERS (cont.)...

Treasure Antique Shows-Benna Voytilla
P.O. Box 9513, Scottsdale, AZ 85251
941-5131

Valley of the Sun Antique Dealers Association
C/O 516 S. Mill Ave., Tempe, AZ 85281
967-4729
See ad page 103.

ANTIQUE SHOWS...

OCTOBER 4-6, 1985-Tucson
Acorn Antique Guild
Ramada-Tucson
St. Mary's exit and freeway.

OCTOBER 12-13, 1985-Phoenix
Arizona Depression Glass Club
The Travel Lodge
3333 E. Van Buren

OCTOBER 18-20, 1985-Phoenix
6th Annual Phoenix Art Museum Estate Sale
Phoenix Art Museum

NOVEMBER 9, 1985-Phoenix
Arizona Depression Glass Club Flea Market
V.F.W. Hall
4853 E. Thomas

NOVEMBER 29-DECEMBER 1, 1985-Scottsdale
Acorn Antique Guild
Safari Convention Center
4611 W. Scottsdale Rd.

DECEMBER 27-29, 1985-Scottsdale
Valley of the Sun Antique Dealers Assoc. 2nd Annual Show
Safari Convention Center
4611 N. Scottsdale Rd.

JANUARY 3-5, 1986-Wickenburg
Acorn Antique Guild
Community Center, Apache & Valentine St.

JANUARY 3-6, 1986-Yuma
Southwest Antique Guild
Yuma Civic & Convention Center
1440 Desert Hills Dr.

JANUARY 10-12, 1986-Scottsdale
Southwest Antique Guild
Safari Inn Resort
4611 N. Scottsdale Rd.

SOUTHWEST ANTIQUE GUILD

Managers:
Marvin & Marian Little

P.O. Box 3535
West Sedona, Arizona 86340

602/282-3153

1986 SHOW SCHEDULE

Yuma, Arizona
Yuma Civic and Convention Center
1440 Desert Hills Dr.
Jan 3,4,5

Scottsdale, Arizona
Safari Inn Resort
4611 Scottsdale Rd. North
Jan. 10,11,12

Tucson, Arizona
Ramada Inn
404 North Freeway
Jan. 24,25,26

Mesa, Arizona
Mesa Community Center
Centennial Hall
201 North Center St.
Feb. 7,8,9

San Angelo, Texas
San Angelo Convention Center
500 Rio Concho Dr.
Feb 14,15,16

Galveston, Texas
The Moody Center
2100 Seawall Blvd.
Feb. 21,22,23

Fredericksburg, Texas
Pioneer Pavilion
Lady Bird Johnson Community Park
Feb. 28, Mar. 1,2

McAllen, Texas
Holiday Inn
2nd St. and Expressway 83
Mar. 7,8,9

Temple, Texas
Civic Auditorium
3303 North 3rd
Mar. 14,15,16

Wichita Falls, Texas
Woman's Forum
2120 Speedway
Mar. 20,21,22
(This is a Thur., Fri., Sat. show)

Santa Fe, New Mexico
Sweeny Convention Center
201 West Marcy Street
Mar. 28,29,30

Flagstaff, Arizona
Sedona, Flagstaff Symphony League
Antique Show-Sale
Little America
July 11,12
Fri., Sat. show

A Friendly Warning!

DON'T MISS The Best ANTIQUE SHOW & SALE! Coming Soon

The Valley of the Sun Antique Dealers Association

Presents its 2nd Annual

HOLIDAY EXTRAVAGANZA!

THE 'SMART' 'CHIC' 'SNAPPY' SHOW!

December 27, 28, 29, 1985

Friday 11-9   Saturday 11-7   Sunday 11-5

Scottsdale Safari Inn

4611 North Scottsdale Road

Over 40 Dealers from Coast to Coast

VALUABLE DOOR PRIZES!

Admission $2.50 all three days. 50¢ discount coupons available at member shops.

ANTIQUE SHOWS (cont.)...

JANUARY 24-26, 1986-Tucson
Southwest Antique Guild
Ramada Inn
404 N. Freeway

FEBRUARY 7-9, 1986-Mesa
Southwest Antique Guild
Centennial Hall, Mesa Community Center
201 N. Center St.

FEBRUARY 14-16, 1986-San Angelo, TX
Southwest Antique Guild
San Angelo Convention Center
500 Rio Concho Dr.

FEBRUARY 21-23, 1986-Galveston, TX
Southwest Antique Guild
The Moody Center
2100 Seawall Blvd.

FEBRUARY 28-MARCH 2, 1986-Fredericksburg, TX
Southwest Antique Guild
Pioneer Pavilion
Lady Bird Johnson Community Park

FEBRUARY 28-MARCH 2, 1986-Phoenix
Acorn Antique Guild
Arizona State Fairgrounds
1826 W. McDowell

MARCH 7-9, 1986-McAllen, TX
Southwest Antique Guild
Holiday Inn
2nd St. & Expressway 83.

March 8-9, 1986-Phoenix
Arizona Depression Glass Club

MARCH 14-16, 1986-Temple, TX
Southwest Antique Guild
Civic Auditorium
3303 N. 3rd

ANTIQUE SHOWS (cont.)...

MARCH 20-22, 1986-Wichita Falls, TX
Southwest Antique Guild
Women's Forum
2120 Speedway

MARCH 28-30, 1986-Santa Fe, NM
Southwest Antique Guild
Sweeny Convention Center
201 W. Marcy St.

APRIL 11-13, 1986-Yuma
Acorn Antique Guild
Convention Center
1440 Desert Hills Dr.

May, 1986-Phoenix
Arizona Depression Glass Club Flea Market

MAY 2-4, 1986-Scottsdale
Acorn Antique Guild
Safari Convention Center
4611 N. Scottsdale Rd.

JUNE 6-8, 1986-Flagstaff
Acorn Antique Guild
North Activity Center
Northern Arizona University

JULY 11-12, 1986-Flagstaff
Sedona, Flagstaff Symphony League Antique Show-Sale
Southwest Antique Guild
Little America

AUGUST, 1986-Prescott
Acorn Antique Guild
Old Armory Building
800 E. Gurley

SEPTEMBER 6-7, 1986-Jerome
Annual 2 Day Jerome Antique Show & Sale
Jerome Chamber of Commerce
Lawrence Hall

INDEX-Locator Maps

INDEX-Dealers & Promoters...

INDEX-Dealers & Promoters (cont.)..

INDEX-Dealers & Promoters (cont.)..

INDEX-Dealers & Promoters (cont.)..

INDEX-Dealers & Promoters (cont.)..

INDEX-Dealers & Promoters (cont.)..

NOTES...

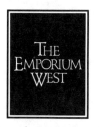